Jonathan Martin

Ansgar Allen

© Ansgar Allen, 2025

ISBN 978-1-7394310-5-1
EQUUS PRESS
Birkbeck College
43 Gordon Square, London, WC1 H0PD, United Kingdom
All rights reserved.
Cover, typeset & design: Interior Ministry
www.equuspress.com

JONATHAN MARTIN

ADVERTISEMENT.

The Author requests his Readers to overlook the many grammatical inaccuracies they are sure to meet with in the following sheets; and he is in hopes of securing their indulgence, when he informs them, that he is only, (as some of them know,) an illiterate man, whose only means of learning was his own unaided efforts, while enduring the confinement he here relates. His aim, in publishing this simple narrative of his life, conversion, and sufferings, is the glory of God, and should it be the means of encouraging one soul to set out for the Kingdom, he will feel amply rewarded.

1

On 27 May 1838, Jonathan Martin lay down and died. It was his fifty-sixth or fifty-seventh year. The bed on which he lay was at the lunatic asylum known as Bethlem, or Bedlam. That evening, another lunatic would take his place, and the room in which he lived would be occupied by another man's thoughts.

This seemed a good place to start. It avoids identifying the beginning of the book with the moment its hero *rises up*. This book will not perpetuate the illusion in which fiction is confused with actuality. It does not start with Jonathan's birth, or even his *most notable achievement*, but mentions it as an aside.

—on 2 February 1829, Jonathan set fire to that noble pile, York Minster, and very nearly destroyed it.

To achieve a total understanding of Jonathan's madness, it would be necessary to give a total account of his experience, a total account of his experience that would be a total derangement. The word *total* should not be misunderstood, the author wrote. It cannot mean a *complete* account, nor can it mean a *comprehensive* account, but a broken one.

No book can deliver his life by accompanying the boy who becomes the boy before the man, the man who was delivered in his delusion to become the man before the lunatic. Even Jonathan could not write such a book or give a verbal account that told of it. There is no telling it.

The boy was tongue-tied. His tie was cut when he was six, but Jonathan carried the effect and spoke with some kind of impediment for the rest of his life. This served to interrupt the flow of his speech. Which reminded the boy, as it would remind the man, of the vast gulf that existed between his so-called inner world and the outer world he grew to deplore, a world that he would have to destroy if it was to be redeemed.

There was the memory of the cut, the doctor wielding a sharp knife, his mouth held open by force—itself a symbol of violent intrusion, the invasion of the world upon his tongue.

The intentions were good enough, but the pain of it flayed those intentions, and all other good intentions too, and the very concept of the good. The tongue was cut, and it suffered, but that cut released the tongue upon its world.

This might be over-reading the event, the author thought, but liking the reading nonetheless, decided to keep it in.

The boy was not schooled and did never learn to properly spell. Although here, his editors and publishers stepped in. The words were made legible and ordinary.

Jonathan's deranged orthographies can only be found in some letters that were quoted verbatim, and his drawings.

Hear the word of the Lord Oh You Blind Hipacrits you Saarpents and Vipears of Hell You wine Bibears and Beffe Yeatears.

—this from a letter written in January 1829, shortly before the fire.

It is the day of vangens and your Cumplet Distructton is at Hand.

—this from a letter written slightly earlier that month.

Ar you not like the man that bilt his hous upon the Sands when the Thunder starmes of Gods Heavye vangens lites upon your Gildrys Heads a way gos your sandey Foundaytons and you to the deepest pet of Hell.

—a little later on in the same letter.

The derangement of Jonathan's mind was extended to the derangement of his words which any reader can suffer who reads those words as they were originally written. The man did not just fail to learn to spell, even if that is how he excused it. His deranged notations were merely words not yet ordered, or domesticated.

The man remained uneducated, he said. This was true to an extent. And it was the basis of his insight.

By remaining uneducated, Jonathan was able to see things the educated can never glimpse.

Jonathan saw the civilized world as it lay, tilted impossibly from its axis and destined in that condition for ruin.

The destruction of the cathedral at York was already immanent within its activities—the rot was set in, and the building and its people condemned. To destroy the Minster by fire could be seen both as a warning and as a realisation.

In writing this book, the author was aware of the influence of style upon the realisation of a life and did attempt a Joycean *Life of Jonathan Martin,* a Woolfian *Life of Jonathan Martin,* and, in turn, a Beckettian *Life of Jonathan Martin.*

That Jonathan's mother was afflicted by strange dreams prior to his birth is not recorded.

Neither is it remarked that no such dreams were had with William, her first child, later known, or wishing to be known, as *The Philosophical Conqueror of All Nations*.

William arrived in 1772. Jonathan in 1782. Plentiful dreams for Jonathan. None, or nothing unusual, for William.

That William's mother dreamt nothing untoward when carrying William surely can be traced to his philosophy, the author wrote, which was odd, certainly, but never otherworldly.

When pregnant with William, she still dreamed of her flight from Lowland's End to Gretna Green. She re-lived her family's disapproval at the sight of the journeyman tanner, his father-to-be. They took off on horseback.

Their mother, this woman, was the daughter of a minor landed proprietor.

Nor did she dream when carrying Richard, her second son, even though he was destined to become a poet. But Richard would also become a Quartermaster-Sergeant, stationed here and there. And this fact—the idiocy of military life—must surely obliterate any residual effect of being a poet.

Richard, the second son, was born at the Brig of Doon, near Ayr.

William, the first son, was born at Haltwhistle, which is the exact centre of the island.

—*Our town lies at the centre of Great Britain*, the boast of more than one place. There are different ways of calculating it.

Richard's date of birth is not recorded. It is only known that Richard came after William and before Jonathan, who was born at Hexham.

Jonathan would become known as the Incendiary, and not the Arsonist, or Firestarter, for instance.

Then came Ann, born at Kilcolemceal. And last of all John, born at Haydon Bridge in 1789. He would become known as the Artist.

It has been noted that all five children were born in different places. There were others too, also born in different places. But they died young.

It has not been noted that there was something odd, if not a little cruel, about naming one child Jonathan and another John. But these names are completely unrelated. One means *given by God*, and the other *graced by God*.

There is always some amount of malice in a gift, it has been said.

The biblical Jonathan was good at slinging rocks; the biblical John was a talent at slinging words. Jonathan was the son of a perverse and rebellious woman. John's mother was related to the holiest woman on earth, by some accounts.

By the time she carried Jonathan, her husband had given up on his prophesies, as she called them. The vast bulk of his foretelling had been expended on their first son.

For William, he prophesied at length. William would achieve this and that and do him this and that great honour. The rest of this foretelling was then offloaded on their second son, Richard.

That was the logic of it—those hopes for greatness that were incompatible with his vision for the first son were expended on his second.

By the time they lived in Hexham, Jonathan's father merely consented to the coming of his existence—Jonathan was at least the third child by this point.

Shortly after his mother died in 1813, aged 52, she appeared to Jonathan in a dream, together with his sister, and told him that he would be hanged. You will hang, she told him, and then vanished from sight.

Years later, he did not hang. Jonathan was declared insane at his trial and so committed to an asylum. He nonetheless lived before the event of his committal as if he would hang. And after his committal, too, he lived like that, it has to be said.

My mother came to me in a dream and told me I will hang, he would tell others. And when she told me that, my sister stood by and there was nothing on her face.

When she carried Jonathan, his mother did not dream of him being hung. This was only Jonathan's dream after she no longer carried him, because she was dead, and Jonathan was a man.

When his mother had Jonathan inside her, she did not dream of her child at all. She was possessed with images of her womb turned inside out and made to carry the ash of the world.

When she carried William, the Philosopher, her dreams were filled with ordinary events. When she carried Richard, the Poet, her dreams were also filled with the everyday. The same went for John, the Artist. Even for John, the Artist, it was all ordinary. Only for Jonathan, the Incendiary, did her dreams have no equivalent in the waking state.

But there was also Ann, who would later play with Jonathan. When she carried Ann, her dreams were plagued with a vertiginous feeling of a womb inside a womb carrying ash.

2

My mother could not suckle me, is what Jonathan Martin wrote in *The Life of Jonathan Martin, Written by Himself.* He writes about that near the end of the book. It was on account of his tongue-tie that she could not do so—as it was later explained—and so he was sent to a nurse. It is not clear what the nurse did that his mother could not do.

This was printed in the *Second Edition, Considerably Improved,* published together with engravings by the author. The same text may have appeared in the first edition.

It does not appear in the *Third Edition, Considerably Improved.* Jonathan no longer writes, or has printed, my mother could not suckle me. By the third edition his suckling, or not suckling, had been edited out.

The full title in each case is *The Life of Jonathan Martin, of Darlington, Tanner. Written by Himself.* The third edition was published in 1828, a year before its author set fire to the cathedral at York. The second edition was published in 1826. This is why the full title did not read, *The Life of Jonathan Martin, Incendiary,* or something like that.

The price of the third edition is listed as sixpence. The book was self-published and hawked about by the author to make a living. There is a curious addendum to the back cover. *N B Gentlemen and Ladies,* it begins, *think it not strange that I charge you one shilling for my Book and the Price on the title only sixpence.* This minor swindle is justified by the line, *for the Lord says remember the poor,* to which is added, *you will find my Book give you satisfaction.* In the old money, one shilling was a fair bit more than sixpence.

The second edition was advertised at eight pence. Which means that the second edition cost more than the third but still less without the swindle. It was printed at Barnard Castle by Thomas Clifton.

Jonathan's life was already worthy of a readership before the fire at York. The third edition advertises his *Providential Escape from the Asylum after being confined three years, through the roof of the House, near Newcastle, having cut his fetters with a sandy stone.* This was the first asylum he was confined to, not to be confused with the second confinement at Bethlem.

The second edition begins its advert by mentioning how often Jonathan has benefited from divine intervention, or the *Extraordinary Interpositions of Divine Providence on his behalf.* These include various close shaves in the navy, and once more his *being locked up in an asylum and ironed,* and his subsequent and *miraculous Escape through the roof of the house.* The same fetters are ground off with the same sandy stone.

The orthography, by the way, is absolutely fine and correct. R.E. Leary or one of his associates might be credited for removing some of the errors. This is because R.E. Leary, at Lincoln, is listed as the printer of the third edition.

Thomas Clifton, printer of the second edition, probably removed more errors than Leary. Most errors were removed in the production of the first, one can assume.

Still, there is an apology in the second edition, which asks the reader to overlook *the many grammatical inaccuracies* because its author is, after all, *an illiterate man.*

His status as an illiterate man has been connected to his belief in the second coming, known as millenarianism, or something like it, that is to say, the Jonathan version of the biblical account of the second coming.

The idea that the world as we know it is about to come to an end, that the reign of the Antichrist is almost over, that the tables will turn and the poor will inherit the earth, is a view from the bottom of the pile. It has been described as the superstition of the uneducated, credulous classes and their associated religions, millenarian sects that flourish in times of uncertainty. It is the ideology of periods of transition. It is the necessarily false yet necessary belief of those who have suffered severe and widespread upheaval, those who can see a part of themselves laid out for annihilation and reach to the Book of Revelation to make sense of it—this, at least, is the judgement made against them, a judgement that is also an explanation, a judgement that disguises itself as explanation.

It is also the context within which Jonathan Martin was seen, in which he appeared as not all that unusual, as another impoverished, illiterate raver with links to Methodism. There was good reason to tread carefully at his trial and not overly insult his religion. Persecuted for his religious ties, he would have become incandescent.

Methodism hardly needed the association. *The Methodists manifest strange aversion to Jonathan Martin being acknowledged as a member of their society, and there has been much shuffling, to palm him, if possible, upon some other body.* This from *The Times* on 10 March 1829. The trial would be later that month.

Jonathan accounts for his childhood in the last pages of the second edition but not the third. The account he gives of his life actually begins in adulthood, at 22, which was when he travelled to London and was press-ganged into the navy.

Or, he mentions he was born. Jonathan says that he was born, gives the year and place, and then, after a line or two, jumps to his 22nd year.

So, his life, *written by himself*, begins by mentioning he was born, jumps swiftly to an account of his adulthood, and then returns eventually to his childhood. Otherwise, it is chronological.

Because he was unable to speak, or not very well, the boy played alone. This is what he writes. The boy spent much of his time wandering in the woods at which his father was a forester.

Jonathan's father held several different jobs over the years. He was also a tanner, for instance.

His father once mentioned that saplings of a certain kind of tree did not belong in the forest, and so Jonathan spent his time looking for trees like that and hacking them down. He would do this with a stick, hacking and hacking at the young tree, which was often merely a few feet high, until the green flesh appeared, and then the yellow woody part, and then straight through. A combination of stamping, further hacking, and kicking was often necessary to fell the thing.

The boy found an old blade in the outhouse, some kind of cutting instrument used by harvesters, or ground clearers, he could not tell. It had a curved nib, like a hook, and a wooden handle. The metal was rusted over. He used that for a week until the blade flew off the handle. It was lodged between his toes. Jonathan lifted his foot, a little bloodied and torn, and left the blade where it stuck in the ground. With the forest as it was, the limping, bloodied boy could not remember where exactly it happened and so never retrieved his superior tool. After that, he returned to the use of sticks against the saplings, and then eventually a broom handle, which was better.

Jonathan's father taught sword and single-stick exercises and kept a public house at one point. That was before William was born.

Their father also enlisted. He left whatever he was doing at the time—working in the tannery, working in the forest—and crossed the Atlantic. The ex-tanner, ex-forester, was soon wounded and pensioned off. The American War of Independence was done with him. There had been fighting, but it was mainly squalid living, setting up camp and seeing each encampment turn the earth over and into the usual liquid filth, the mess they left behind each time they moved on to carry, and haul, and steal cattle, destroy bridges, dam rivers, and so on, and smoke, and talk, and wait for supplies, and watch men die or hobble with the mute stupor of a fresh amputee.

And coachbuilding, he did that too.

At his trial, Jonathan did not walk strangely, or leer about, or seem at all impaired by his madness. His trial was something of a disappointment to those who had come to see a lunatic. As one spectator remarked, the judge with his wig and gouty leg did a better job. But the physicians testified that his gaze was surely that of a monomaniac, even if he did not rave, even if he did not lose his head to the satisfaction of those assembled. The peculiarity of Jonathan Martin was exactly this. When not possessed by his religious fervour, the man seemed entirely in control of his faculties. And yet they had seen him properly, so they said. The physicians had taken the opportunity to inspect the man and brought, as they did, the accumulated knowledge of similar inspections carried out on other similar men. Viewed up close, he was a certifiable lunatic, they said, and that explained it. These physicians told the court how his eyes were often glassy, and red, and dilated, and anyone accustomed with the disease could see its mark.

The author notes that monomania is one of those numerous categories for mental ill-health which has been discarded, so that when a contemporary physician hears of Jonathan's *monomania*, the diagnosis no longer makes any proper sense and his so-called lunacy is no longer assured in the same way.

During one of several attempts to flee the navy, Jonathan lost his trousers. Then he really did walk oddly, or look odd, as a man always does without his trousers, however he manages to walk.

And then there were those times he would walk blindfold towards the lead mines until his sister said, stop. He walked differently then. He was also less than half his height. A child.

But anyone who walks at all must look odd, it has to be said, if the world is really seeing its last days as Jonathan later believed, when nothing but the midnight cry, or last shriek into the abyss of human suffering, can be promised by religion this side of the millennium.

Millenarianism accentuates its perception of destruction—the lived, daily destructions enacted within so-called civilization—and extends that perception to the idea of cosmic destruction. It conceives of a total annihilation, a total annihilation that will at the same time be a total cleansing and a total salvation.

There is no real distinction between secular life and religious belief in a world facing its ruin. The infidel cannot be separated from the faithful and destroyers will not be distinguishable from prophets. Which is another way of saying that daemons walk hand in hand with saints, as Jonathan might have said, leaving the rest with no compass to navigate by, path to follow, or pit to flee for.

William, the Philosopher, knew of his brother's fears and attempted to engage him with the consolations of his craft. I cannot deny, William said, *that the Sun shall be turned into darkness, and the Moon into blood, before the great and terrible day of the Lord cometh.* Because that is how it is written in God's book. But we should not take these words literally, he went on. You have always taken everything literally, he told his brother.

It is probable that this is how it will all look, William said, when the atmosphere of the earth is in flames, and is probable, moreover that this is the fate of all planets, he went on, and not simply our own. But there will be *no celestial blood*, he said, merely celestial fire. It may well be, he continued, that the Most High hath, in his wisdom, decreed a similar fate, the exact same exit, for every one of his heavenly bodies, and that from their remains will spring new worlds and new systems filled with myriads of intelligent beings like ourselves. If destruction cometh from the Lord, why not renovation, and why not that renovation countless times, so that our own destruction and replacement will be nothing in the great scheme of His work.

As a boy, Jonathan acquired the habit of rising at 2am, that specific hour of the night when the day is undecided and when unheard sounds greet that indecision—the growth of the next ring of a tree, the eruption of mud driven by the activity of worms—and points still further from that stillness, and for those who can hear, to the rise and fall of coastlines and their communities, these last outposts of a failing civilization, which set themselves against the persistent aggression of the sea and to those creatures it folds over at its edges. Inland, as the forests retreat, they give up their last, the fog that drifts from the upper branches. The anatomy of the land appears.

Jonathan clambered over the anatomy below and into the forest, between the stumps his father had left to the sun to become bleached or to grow feebly at the edges and from the roots. It was a consequence of his speech impediment and his decision to associate with none other than himself that he took to walking at night, so he said.

His ramblings were eventually stopped when he was brought home by the lead miners, and when his parents finally discovered how the boy wandered every night from that early hour until dawn. This Jonathan returned and fell into his cot to become the boy they did recall seeing, the one they could never easily rouse and would according to their temperament that day leave alone until later, or repeatedly return to and shake, and poke, and talk at, until he stood.

A small boy had recently died, down the mine, as did happen. The conditions for the adults were not particularly good either. They worked along a near-horizontal tunnel, pursuing a seam, and as they worked at the hard face their journey back to the surface increased. Which is to say, their conditions worsened by each foot the tunnel lengthened. On the surface, a foot in length is nothing to think of. In the cramped conditions of the tunnel, a foot means something entirely different. The first foot of a tunnel is indeed a foot, the same foot that can be measured and walked on the surface. Further on, each foot grows and grows until a foot below no longer even remotely resembles a foot above. It cannot even be matched against the foot either side, the foot before it, and the foot that comes after, due to the rate of growth. Each foot is then different, distended from its neighbour.

The more they mined, the further the ore had to be taken, dragged along with all the other rock only good for tipping. And so, ever more effort went into producing what they were paid for by the fixed measure of weight. It was also the case they had no alcove or hollow to retreat to when blasting rock, so the miner who lit it simply crawled as fast as possible and as far as crawling would take him. Sometimes they would make a boy light it and run. A small boy will run along a tunnel an adult can only stoop through. But small boys were unreliable with their footing.

One miner did eventually work for several days without pay to carve out a minor recess with a single-point pick. This recess was then used for shelter until it was too far from the end of the tunnel to be reached in time before the next blast. The legs stuck out, but the body was protected. These were typical calculations—to dig a recess unpaid or continue work at the end of the tunnel for a pittance—and calculations like that were repeated in lead mines elsewhere.

There was midway a natural cavern into which the tunnel emerged and from which it then went on. In that cavern was a pit, and into that pit filled with water at its base they threw what rocks they could hurl that far without falling in themselves. This lessened the work of hauling above for weeks. They thew down what rocks they knew in the feeble light were not rich in lead until the foreman caught them doing it and said they could never really tell, down there, which of the rocks and rubble were no good, and that only in the light of the day would they know, and so they must haul everything to the surface. This lessened the amount they threw into the pit, but still, it went on for weeks. Vast quantities of rock went down, they felt, yet the rock did not fill the pit, and the surface of the water continued to swallow all that hit it.

Everything down there was given a name, including the pit. In doing so, they drew from the most daemonic imaginings in their lexicon. Even the side recess into which they fled was further darkened by the name they gave it. These words were murmured below and never taken to the surface.

When Jonathan appeared on the rise above the mine entrance shortly before dawn, they thought him to be a ghost—the boy that died. Then he walked towards them, and they saw he was another boy. When asked what he was doing there, the boy told them he wished to see them go underground. I want to see how it looks when you go in, he said, and the entrance takes you and turns entirely black.

The miners asked him whom he belonged to. This was because the boy did not yet belong to himself and the name Jonathan

Martin still meant nothing. Even to his parents he was merely Jon. Parents vested differently in their children when they died so readily, as his siblings had and would.

Their work underground had not yet started and the men were still shifting rubble from the day before. One took the boy home. The distance, measured in feet, was comparably nothing to walk, and the foreman had not yet arrived.

And so it was, Jonathan's parents were woken from sleep by the miner who hammered the front door, still holding his lamp, and the boy who did not belong to himself was returned.

Jon admitted to his parents that he roamed every night. It was not drawn out, the information. The boy plainly said this is what he did, and he had been doing it for as long as he could think.

Afterwards, his parents made sure the door was bolted each night, and the windows too. From then on, young Jonathan walked about his room.

There were other events too that marked his childhood and the memory of which he carried forward. Such as the time he fell headfirst into a trough and could not get free. His sister pulled him out by the feet. That was Ann, most probably, but it could have been one of the others, one of those who would only know childhood and would only see bucolic images like that, like a brother stuck feet upwards in a trough.

Or a brother limping into the house with a bloodied foot after the incident with the sapling.

3

Jonathan had a son. His son was called Richard. This boy did eventually belong to himself more than most people ever manage to belong to themselves. Most people live by fleeing themselves and not by taking hold of their being, tightly taking hold of it, and extinguishing it.

Richard took his own life after his father died in the asylum in 1838. Three months later, apparently, and it was an awful suicide, they said.

He was named Richard, and not Jonathan, after his father. His father felt that the Christian name that he had been given had only brought him bad luck.

When Jonathan was committed to the asylum in 1829, Richard, aged 15, went to live with his uncle, John Martin.

John, the Artist, had become obsessed, like William the Philosopher, with inventing machines that would solve all problems. He wore himself out devising Elastic Iron Ships and other such things, fearful, again like William, that everything he invented would be stolen from him and others would profit from his genius.

By 1838, John Martin felt himself a ruined man, and the boy he had taken under his wing was soon ruined too. Richard said that he could see his breath as it emerged from his mouth and that his breath wrapped around all who came near him, turning them black. His aunt sent for the doctor, and some vial of some sort was prescribed. Otherwise, they endured it because Richard was more often silent, contemplating his visions, perhaps, or retreating into vacancy, he was never invited to tell.

John, the Artist, did not retreat into vacancy. He remained possessed, and he died possessed. William, the Philosopher, the other uncle, did not retreat into vacancy either. The *Philosophical Conqueror of all Nations* was not permitted to do so.

That was the title of one of William's last self-published books and one of his last gifts to humanity.

Anyone who knew him must know it, he thought. A true philosopher does not permit himself rest from his thinking. Any thought, however reduced or fruitless, can be refined, or it can be replaced by another thought which might be better. This was how William approached the problem of invention. Even as everything he invented was stolen from him—testimony to the potency of his mind—he could not rest from inventing something else and then something else since that is what a philosopher does. A prolific philosopher like himself sheds ideas like he sheds his hair.

He designed a boat on the principle of a swan's foot, for instance.

And a new principle of architecture by a slight dovetail. Again, he was the one who contrived it—I invented this too, he said. His mind was profligate in its generosities.

When William was very little, he lived in the mountains with his grandparents. They had been recruited to show the Highlanders how to cultivate their land.

There were no fences, and the eagles and ravens laid their eggs on cliffy rocks. They caused great destruction during the lambing season, he said. The boy William was recruited to tear about between the ewes to protect the lambs when the shepherds were elsewhere, but he amused his *little mind* instead with climbing the elevations, eating the berries which grew in great abundance, and getting swallowed from the vantage of the upper horizons along the various burns, and becks, and their minor valleys which were full of trout and which he could take out by the hand if he tickled them the right way.

William himself referred to his mind, back then, as his *little mind*. Another symptom of his intellectual growth, perhaps.

Not understanding Gaelic, but with the shepherd knowing English, little William was tricked into believing that all the children who surrounded him in those parts were insulting his country and his countrymen and that when they addressed him they never wished to communicate anything but contempt. It was not their contempt, of course, but the shepherd's, who was old enough to hate the English and despise his employer, the boy's grandfather. This shepherd knew to hate the Englishman who felt that he had something to teach. The shepherd's contempt was shared by many others too, who ensured that the Englishman was met with scorn by all who encountered him, in those parts, even if that scorn was mainly hidden and then directed into other channels, such as tormenting the young William.

When William found out, he threatened to tell his grandmother, which put a stop to it, because the shepherd still wished to eat.

This is not to say the Highland children could not feel contempt or originate their own, even if the contempt of children for one another is more often than not acquired from the adults in their company.

The land was owned, and the sheep were already spoken for. Soon, there would be enclosures and fences. But for the moment, those who lived on the land and had lived there before the English teachers of land cultivation arrived thought of the terrain they inhabited in the old way. Sheep Island, nearby to where William lived, *was an island that might feed two persons very soon fat, but regarding three, would hardly keep them.*

Two or three hundred yards from Sheep Island lies the Isle of Sanday belonging to the Laird of Sanday. The Lairds were a problem as well as the English. But the Isle had several small coves that were ideal for smuggling and that the Laird did not know about. The rocks in the cliffs also contained many small holes where goods might be stowed. The Laird did not know about them either. The land above was tolerably good, which was the Laird's understanding too. It defined how much profit he felt that he might extract from the soil.

A few hundred yards further lies the rock of Dunaverty. It has a flat top, and that top is fairly difficult to get up to, even despite the track which is steep enough to put off the casual walker. The rock is famous for a battle fought atop it during which many were thrown off the sides.

William thought often about the battle at Dunaverty, particularly about men falling off its sides. He thought about how they must have looked and sounded. The boy climbed those minor rocks that are strewn between the blueberries, the heather, and the gorse, and re-enacted the entire siege, a lengthy dramatic production that consumed all his attention and to which he devoted himself when he was not saving the lambs from the eagles and the ravens. These were the two top predators now that the foxes were gone and the mountain cat no longer existed.

The foxes and cats had recently been destroyed by two hunters. The Duke of Argyle had sent the men, but they were sustained from the larders of the peninsular dwellers. The farmers were expected to house the hunters too, whose work produced—so they declared—ungodly thirsts and appetites.

William recalled how the small terriers these men hunted with were torn about their heads and jaws from fighting the foxes in their holes. These terriers also required meats, and looked to the farmers for it, like their masters.

It might have been cheaper and quieter to let the foxes and the mountain cat have an occasional lamb to eat.

The boy William was also preoccupied with thinking about the entrance at Piper's Cove, said to convey those who let it swallow them into a labyrinth 15 miles in length and somewhat more in distance trod, which would take anyone who entered it, and who had the stamina, to another part of the country. William himself often went to the cove and stood at the dark mouth of the labyrinth, terrorizing himself as little boys do with the thought of going in.

The piper never came out. He entered with his dog, and his pipes, and so many candles as he thought he would need, and the people said that only his dog emerged, several days later, entirely bald.

Jonathan never saw Piper's Cove, but his brother told him about it. His brother also told Ann, and John, and Richard the future Poet and Quartermaster-Sergeant, and some of the other siblings too.

His siblings also heard about Dunaverty Rock, which William claimed to have ascended, and the ancient bones he saw on the ledges in the sides of the cliffs that the younger ones mixed in their minds with the lambs William also went on about. These he found after they had been attacked and disembowelled by the birds when he was away picking berries, or re-enacting the battle, or staring into the void at Piper's Cove.

The piper only entered the cave because he laid a wager. He would go in at one end and emerge somewhere else altogether.

Wagers are the root of idiotic commitments—they are too easily said. A better wager would be one that ties the ordeal it imagines into the speaking act of the wager itself.

About 5 miles inland is a limestone quarry. Someone heard the sound of the piper's pipes drifting up from it, so they said. Perhaps through a crack that let into its sides and connected to the cavern below. It was the Highland tune with the words, *magela, magela, magela mage,* which William understood to mean, I will never, I will never, I will never return.

William also told his siblings about the witch who threatened the local tailor that she would flee with him on her back to Ireland and would fly so high that his bonnet would touch the ceiling of it.

Sometimes, William told the story a little differently, with the two figures arranged in reverse as they flew, so it was the witch who flew on the tailor's back rather than the tailor on the witch. That would make the tailor her stick.

He also told them how respected their grandfather was among the locals and how they would bring swine's flesh to his house from all parts of the country. Not a week would pass, he said to his siblings, without some swine's flesh delivered to the door. There were days when the stuff was piled up, they had a barrow for it in the yard, and as you left the house, there was the unmistakable smell, frequently whole pigs, but sometimes also hacked into pieces for ease of transport. That is how the Highlanders respected him, William said. They read in the Bible that pig should not be eaten and this lesson affected them in some basic way, but still valuing the pigs they farmed, they took them to the one person they valued above all others on the peninsula. The same Highlanders did not subsequently read how Christ did away with the idea of not eating pig in the very same book, and their grandfather was too polite to say. He cured it all instead, William told his siblings, using the English method, and made great profit because of the amount of swine delivered. William said he had seen as many swine cheeks in the house as would load a cart, and that these cheeks were of the finest kind, and the meat dried to a nicety, and they had plenty of milk, butter, and cheese in the house as a result, and all the offals too that were hung up like curtains, he said, because his grandfather's house was most probably one of the finest meat houses in Scotland.

The duke's hunters certainly regarded his grandfather with special affection due to the abundance of meat about the house. William said he never saw the duke's men visit because the foxes were largely defeated and the mountain cat was already gone by the time he lived there, but that several severed feet remained, and one or two tails, given by the hunters as tokens of appreciation, he was told. Otherwise, their grandfather lived in the English fashion, William said, and did not stop living in the English fashion despite the length of time spent living alongside those who lived differently. It came with many dainties, William recalled.

William repeated the name of their grandfather. He repeated that name in front of his siblings who did not know their grandfather as he had done, and as William said that name, he did so very grandly, enunciating the name of their grandfather very precisely, both names with equal attention, and told them too that when his wife, their grandmother, died, she gave prophecy to her nurse, on her own deathbed, that his great name would one day sound from Pole to Pole, which the author found to be true to the extent that William's recollections were later, much later, digitized, and sent electronically.

William said their grandfather was much bewailed and lamented upon his burial in Cambletown, and by rich and poor alike, because of the respect he was owed, and so on, even if he was secretly much despised, as the story of the shepherd indicates.

His family and their servants prayed twice a day after that, and all neighbours who could attend these lamentations did so too, and they were still praying 50 years later, apparently, which is when William sets down these recollections in one of the many pamphlets he had printed, at his own expense, and attempted to sell to anyone who came near, mainly on the streets in Newcastle where he lived and grew old and was tolerated as an oddity by the locals. This pamphlet, published in 1833, was entitled in the old way, that is to say, at great length—*A Short Outline of the Philosopher's Life, from being a child in frocks to this present day, after the Defeat of Impostors, False Philosophers, since the Creation.*

By the Will of the Mighty God of the Universe, it continues, *he has Laid the Grand Foundation for Church Reform by True Philosophy.*

And the title goes on—*All my inventions, which would make a large volume, are not named, as it would put it out of the reach of the poorer classes of people to purchase.*

And finally, *the burning of York Minster is not left out, and an account of four brothers and one sister.*

The bit about York Minster probably caused annoyance. The fire was not four years old and the Minster had not long been repaired. Probably it still smelt a bit, inside, of the conflagration.

Shortly before their grandmother died, she mentioned that William, the first born, had a God-like soul. This was something William frequently told to his brothers and sisters. Our grandmother saw that I had a God-like soul, he said to them. And shortly before she passed, she heard heavenly music when thinking about that. She thought about my God-like soul and heard heavenly music, he said. But then, fearing that the sounds she heard were not of heaven and that the music was an intrusion and a deception, she decided not to wake us all so that we could hear it too. This caused them some mirth, Ann, John, Richard the future Poet and Quartermaster-Sergeant, and Jonathan too, and the other siblings then living all laughing, and so William said, *despite her doubts about the music, she had no doubts about my soul.* You may laugh about the heavenly music, but you cannot laugh when it comes to what she said about my heavenly soul. She told her nurse she had no doubts about it, and her nurse came to me and said despite what she feared in relation to the music, there was no doubt concerning her conviction in relation to the God-like nature of her grandson.

Ann, John, Richard, Jonathan, and the other siblings then living, went on and on about the heavenly music and would not let it rest. William decided it was most likely the piper in his pit and that this accounted for the noise.

William also fancied himself as a poet. He wrote a long and artless poem about his brother Jonathan and how he had triumphed at York in burning down the establishment. There was a much shorter one devoted to his grandmother, in which William describes her as an angel. The woman is conveyed to Heaven very straightforwardly, as was her due. With her soul so quickly and happily sublimated, William devotes the rest of the verse to thinking about the fate of her body and the vile terrestrial earth it was left to moulder in. These are his words. The wicked, he declares, have no such luck, since they take their vile bodies with them, polluting those dark regions the damned are sent to with further putrefaction. Somehow, the poem remains cheery, although another reader, and here the author might be included, may view this preoccupation with the body of his grandmother as a perverse and telling intrusion.

Jonathan's soul could not be described as God-like since his soul, like everything else, was already fallen. This soul, like every other, was facing its destruction besides. To describe anything as God-like on this here earth, at that point in history, during the reign of the Antichrist, was a dangerous or telling delusion.

Or so a millenarian might think. And if Jonathan was a millenarian, he might have thought that too.

No souls are good here on earth, or if they are good, they are only good in the relative sense that some souls are less possessed of evil than others.

In the grand scheme of things, that makes all possible souls existing on earth, not particularly good.

So, William would have been right, or less wrong, if he had written, *my grandmother believed I was not as much possessed of the devil as another child of the more regular variety, and of whom one might not so easily remark that this or that child had a God-like soul.*

Actually, it would have been much simpler to write, *all children are pretty much as fallen as most adults.* Or, more simply still, *there is the devil in us all.*

If Jonathan could not see himself as God-like and excluded from his delusions the possibility of his own saintliness, he did have powers of discernment. Jonathan mentions that God created four brothers. God has raised us four brothers, Jonathan writes—listing the achievements of himself, John, and William—forgetting for a moment his sister, Ann, and the other siblings too. Even if they were only half raised and so only half existed, they might still be half mentioned, one would think, or so the author feels.

He also neglected to mention the achievements of his second-born brother, Richard the Quartermaster-Sergeant. Here, Jonathan seems to conspire with the other two brothers in making so little known about his life.

4

Richard was at Waterloo, this much is known about him, but that could mean almost anything.

The most detail to be had about Richard comes in his *Last Days of the Antediluvian World*, including also *A Forlorn Hope* and *Ishmael's Address*.

2600 lines of highfalutin blank-verse drivel. Again, self-published.

The notable thing about Richard is that his sympathy is with Ishmael, the outcast, a wild donkey of a man, and not with Abraham, for instance, who is a tyrant, or Jacob, who is a vile deceiver.

Richard was a bit like John, the Artist, who also liked to defile biblical heroes. Or perhaps Richard imitated John in that respect. Or maybe John imitated Richard, which might explain why John says so little about him.

As John, the Artist, liked to declaim, David was a cruel monster, Jacob was a thief, and Moses a murderer, or Moses was at least an incompetent who should have gotten the Jews through the wilderness in just a few days. He took far too long at it, and so he was a murderer.

Or perhaps he was a murderer for keeping on bothering the Pharaoh, demanding their freedom, and prompting yet another plague and killing spree as a demonstration of God's wrath.

The plague of frogs, the plague of gnats. Necessary cleansing.

Depending how one looks at it, the murderer of one people becomes the saviour of the next. When everything is fallen, the murderer holds the highest office.

Jonathan was more respectful of God's message but less of himself. My eldest brother, God has made a natural philosopher, Jonathan writes, and my youngest an historical painter revered by Kings and Emperors. And I, the unworthiest, God has given me the gift of prophecy.

In his case prophecy meant that everything, or at least the establishment, needs to burn.

And all the efforts of civilization have ultimately come to nought, and so deserve to burn.

And we are living the *Last Days,* to borrow words from Richard, which is when everything burns.

Moses also murdered an Egyptian. And so it is plain enough to describe him as a murderer. John, the Artist, was merely stating facts. It was possible for him to say Moses was a murderer without any judgement at all. The word, murderer, is entirely shorn of any evaluative content when John says it. Or if not entirely shorn, comically shorn, or shorn to comic effect. The word, murderer, is comically shorn of evaluative content when John says it. Because Moses murdered an Egyptian, John rendered the word neutral, or apparently neutral, for comic effect.

To claim neutrality for the word may be too much, but it is surely correct to say Moses took all the negativity from the word *murderer*. Moses left only the positive content of the word behind when he killed the Egyptian.

The fire at York was only the beginning. There will be fires in London, great fires that will spread from its cathedrals and its churches first until all of England moves to collapse at its centre. The land will hoist to right and then to left, and the Union Jack will turn upside down and drag all remaining traces of the land below. Or so Jonathan prophesied.

Jonathan will arrive as the son of Napoleon might do and will stride mightily across the channel. Or it will be the son himself who shall convey such havoc that none would be able to tell the difference between natural cataclysm and the ruins of battle.

The confusion will travel. Jonathan did at times struggle to tell the difference between himself and the son of Napoleon.

The king of England and his drunken priests and bishops will exhale wine underneath the feet of Jonathan, or the son of Napoleon, as those feet press downward, he said.

They will look like fountains.

Prayer books shall turn to pulp between his toes.

All will see they are the causes of their own calamity.

In this, clairvoyance must be practised. Failure at prediction will be endured so as to perfect the art of confident suggestion.

Like when he walked blindfold among the lead mines until his sister said, Oh brother, there is a pit before you. He was already practising then, one might say, and failing but for his sister.

Not long after the two children had another go, this time walking without a blindfold, yet still heedlessly given the terrain. They found themselves falling, her first and then him right after. The opening was covered with turf, which slowed things a bit and gave Jonathan the time and wit to take proper hold either end, on one end his sister, on the other some kind of handhold, and thereby haul them both, each scrambling most likely. His sister did more to rescue them in her memory than she did in his, the siblings glad enough to survive the pit as it was very deep. It would have been a terrible death, they both agreed, a very terrible death, they repeated as they retreated together towards surer ground. They concealed the extent of their terror, cut and bruised in various places and beginning eventually to submit to uncontrollable tremors.

After that, they left the woods for Hexham. Little Jonathan dreamt he was quarrelling with some boys and struck his mother heavily until she woke. He would not be pacified until he was properly returned from his dreaming state to consciousness of the bed in which the family slept. Then Jonathan was put to bed alone for further dreaming.

From behind his sleep, the boy heard a heavy foot come to the chamber door, and three heavy groans, and the door opening and them entering, and his retreating but not his retreating, and a flash of light that illuminated the room and him too. It was a burst of black powder but smokeless, he might have said. More like a thunder strike but inside and with no sound—as he might have described it further—after which they vanished.

This foretold the death of his sister, not Ann, but one of the others, for shortly after she was murdered. The family had good reason to reflect, looking back, he thought, that Jonathan had indeed slept badly some nights before and had told them of his dreams and his fear those dreams foretold something bad—what he did not specify—and that this something bad would come to the family very soon, which it did.

When Jonathan was visited in the asylum following the fire at York, he had attained the status of a curiosity. His freely drawn pictures were much sought after. Jonathan himself recalls he had not shaken so many hands as he had in those last years of his life when so many came to see him in his cell. But he had not for all that attained the status of a prophet.

The difference between a prophet and a lunatic can be measured by the difference between a crowd of followers and a crowd of spectators. Jonathan managed to assemble spectators and not followers.

The same week of Jonathan's dream his sister, not Ann but a different one, was violently thrown down some stone stairs. The woman who did it was brought out by the sound of two girls who had been quarrelling with two boys. The woman, Peggy, emerged, seized my sister—the boys had run away—and threw her. Another neighbour heard the little girl tumble and the noise she made with it and came out yelling all sorts at Peggy but the little girl begged her, Oh Dolly, she said, don't tell my mother, don't tell my mother, she repeated. Don't tell Mother that Peggy threw me lest she thought it well deserved. Her sufferings were very great, writes Jonathan, during the few days that she lived, and her destroyer passed it off very well until the girl was buried, after which the woman was compelled to confess that she, Peggy, was the one who threw the child, and was committed to prison where she subsequently died a miserable death, so he said, or so the family told themselves, having heard that she died, and assuming it was more than ordinarily miserable, their consolation. And she died miserably, they would say, leaving the children wondering what might be more miserable than what they had witnessed.

Their mother instructed them well in their fear of God, or, at least, the teaching of that fear had been passed well enough to Jonathan, who recalls the lesson she taught, that there is a God to serve and a hell to shun, and that all liars and swearers—as she said when they went on with their lying and when they went on with their swearing—are burnt in hell with the Devil and his angels. This caused him to think, pretty much as soon as his sister had fallen and then again when she suffered and more again once she died, that she must surely have sinned something terrible to be thrown like that for no apparent reason.

It is hard to know how to take that lesson, not knowing how their mother said it—if she said it at all—this thing about them joining all liars and swearers to burn in hell. It may have been delivered with tender inflexions, perhaps even deliberate affection, as she remonstrated her children for their little lies and their little curses so that all of what she spoke were the familiar words of their God-fearing milieu, the ordinary words of the violent mythology that all children, like them, were set to inhabit, back then.

This reminds the author how, in another book, the same author, or a relatable author, once wrote about the word *milieu* and about it being detestable. And here it is deployed after all.

The word *milieu* is a little too young to carry the weight of the Norman Conquest and the dominance of courtly life by its linguistic import. But, to the author, that word and others like it still signify the retained conceits of so-called higher culture and educated life. To the author, the word *milieu* is a sign of a self-satisfied, self-regarding pride.

The death of my sister made this country irksome to me, was how Jonathan put it. Fortunately, he was sent off to be his uncle's shepherd near the Roman Wall. This was the one Hadrian built, or had others build to keep out the so-called barbarians, but which functioned as little more than a series of customs posts. After that, Hadrian's Wall soon became the rim of a long and rotting toenail.

The Wall suited my mind very well, Jonathan claimed, and allowed me to retreat into its solitudes. After that I was apprenticed to a tanner, my father having told me it was not bad work, which is true, to an extent, but only after the sight of vats and the smell of their contents has become familiar, and finally mundane, because the body will accustom to any bad smell, just as the civilized have become accustomed to their own odours, and have finally come to believe in themselves.

During these wanderings, Jonathan also contemplated the extraordinary number of Roman penises carved into the wall.

The woods near the tannery were good and deep. Jonathan resumed his habit of retiring to them, the same habit, pretty much, just without the killing of saplings. He thwacked at the nettles instead. This was not yet prophecy.

The difference between a lunatic and a priest may be measured along the same line as between a prophet and a priest. Each speaks from a place beyond established structures. The source of authority for the prophet and for the lunatic is external and not sanctioned by existing orders of meaning.

The priest is confined to the work of commentary, where all miracles and all revelations are essentially sealed off and put out of reach, having occurred so long ago that they are at once ancient and outside of history. The lunatic and the prophet act on the contrary impulse and defy the sclerotic effect of tradition on thought, which insists that each new message issues from an older message, which becomes its referent and guarantor of sense.

A prophet's message and a lunatic's message may take different forms. It may reside in a word, a gesture, an act or a decision not to act, or a determination to remain silent when words are expected.

A new priest emerged with the rise of the first itinerant methodisms, combining the lunatic with the prophet. When methodism was later organised and became an institution like any other, it effectively incorporated lunacy and prophecy within its operations. Which is to say, lunacy and prophecy were disguised and subsumed.

The most difficult message for the prophet is to announce the end of things, that everything is fallen, and nothing can be done. This is the work of the millenarian prophet in its worst, most wretched form.

A prophet who determines to remain silent before apocalypse might argue that anything else is desecration. To speak, even worse, to appear to speak well, is an extension of a fallen world, an act of high barbarism. But none of this can be said by the silent prophet, and so the argument is moot.

A prophet who determines to speak of the end will be treated as an outsider, someone who is beyond the pale, or as a lunatic. But the best accusation is to declare the prophet a barbarian of sorts—*you are against culture, against reason, against the world we know*—so that the prophet can clear things up and argue by reply that barbaric speech is the only kind available, really, and that it would be an act of idiocy to think oneself above it, just as it is an act of idiocy to speak it.

And that barbaric thought, selected, chosen, and deliberately practised, is the best, the most honest form of reason, so-called.

And that a deliberate, barbaric outlook is the only point from which the prophet can speak in order to escape an overly regulated and closed imaginary.

To be identified as a barbarian, or a lunatic, from the perspective of that closed imaginary, is merely the consequence of a barbarian society, a society blind to its own lunacy—the barbarian adds. These words just swing back on themselves.

Jonathan was declared insane at his trial and so allowed to live because he was a lunatic and not a prophet. He never forgave Richard the Quartermaster-Sergeant for arranging this diagnosis as his defence. As a lunatic, he could be excused. As a prophet, he would have been executed—or, more precisely, he would have been executed as a false prophet.

There is a long tradition of identifying and executing false prophets. There is no similar tradition for false lunatics.

A false prophet appears in Revelation, for instance. Spirits looking much like frogs come out of the false prophet's mouth, and there is the usual burning of the false prophet in a lake of fire and brimstone.

The medical term used to explain Jonathan's so-called lunacy, his monomania, describes his fixations—the visions that possessed him—and would explain how, when not possessed, Jonathan was able to function and pass as an ordinary human being.

This accounted for the evidence, the considerable confusion between witnesses, with some declaring that Jonathan was insane, and others declaring he functioned perfectly well, at least as they recollected him.

One point of amusement is that those who hated Jonathan most testified to his lunacy, whereas those more favourably disposed testified to his sanity. His enemies saved him where his friends would have had him killed. A trial of this sort was one of the first of its kind, which is how they might be excused for blundering.

5

In 1724, Edward Arnold was found guilty of shooting, but not quite managing to kill a certain Lord Onslow.

At his trial, the jury was told that for acquittal on grounds of insanity, the accused must be judged to have the mental faculties of a child, or of a brute, a wild beast perhaps. It was not important to decide which, for there is little between them.

Arnold consumed a good amount of drink before the crime, it was noted, during which he was heard complaining that Onslow was in his belly.

Lord Onslow is sat right inside my belly, Arnold was heard to say, clutching his stomach with one hand, holding his drink with the other. I drink, he said, and Lord Onslow takes every drop of it for his self.

The man feared, moreover, that Onslow was deploying imps against him and that Onslow was the source of his boils, and so on.

To acquit this man, the judge said, you must determine that he is totally deprived of his understanding and cannot organise his mind, that he suffers recollections as if they were events, that he lives as an infant encounters the world with heedless emotion, that he has risen no higher in his knowledge of reason and his appreciation of the difference between good and evil than a creature of the forests or the marshes which proceeds from one thing to the next on the basis of its impulses and appetites.

With these words, or something like them, the judge established a legal standard known as the *wild beast test*, which Arnold, for his part, woefully failed. There was still too much reason mixed in with his insanity, they decided.

The would-be regicide, James Hadfield, was deemed insane upon his trial in 1800. This Hadfield had suffered repeated sabre cuts to the head during the French Revolutionary Wars, and those sabre cuts were taken as the cause of it.

For Hadfield, things had changed. It was only thought necessary to establish Hadfield was deluded when he did it, rather than a regular 24/7 wild beast.

Thanks to Hadfield and other unfortunates, by Jonathan's trial the test of lunacy was more specific to his state of mind during the criminal act. It was to establish whether or not he was capable of losing his faculties to such an extent that, when possessed by his fervour, he no longer knew right from wrong.

It was pointed out that Jonathan fled the scene as a criminal might. Had he not known right from wrong at the time, so it was said, Jonathan would not have fled.

When incarcerated, Jonathan lived a cycle of desiring drawing materials and, being given those materials, working himself into a frenzy, and then being deprived of the very activity which had created that frenzy—his drawing and his painting. It was noted that his drawing and his painting made his condition worse, it encouraged him to indulge his fixations. Doing his art brought out his monomania, as they still called it. Each time Jonathan was given his requested materials, the monomania repeated. This cycle helped re-affirm the correctness of his imprisonment.

Subsequent to Hadfield's committal—following his attempted regicide—his drinking partner, Bannister Truelock, was incarcerated too. Both of them resided at Bethlem, the very same asylum that Jonathan would later attend.

Truelock, the cobbler, was another millenarian prophet. This one had been pregnant with the Messiah for the last quarter century. He told Hadfield all about it, about how the Messiah would eventually emerge from his mouth, wafting out as spirit— Hadfield thought perhaps the nostrils too—during which great event, or sometime thereabouts, Truelock would depose the King and set himself down to rule in his place.

All of that became mixed together in Hadfield's skull. It happened as he sat alongside Truelock in the various public houses they moved between, this Hadfield who had been hit too many times about the head and was carved to bits inside as out. They said that Truelock incited Hadfield to kill the King, and that he decided on that once he saw the scars. Having seen the scars he thought, you will be good for inciting.

Truelock's room was at the top of the house. He had coal and candle, which signified comfortable lodgings, and the privilege, as it was put, of mending the inmates' shoes. All of them knew he was bred a shoemaker, as they said, and gave him the opportunity of enjoying his profession. When not mending, or taking the fine view of the Surrey hills—Truelock surveyed that county by standing on a chair that was stood on a table—the cobbler covered the walls of his cell with his prophecies. He kept a large number of canary birds to observe those lines as they were written, which he let in and out of their cages to mix, multiply, and be sold. The Messiah will be born from my mouth, he told all who would listen and kept telling them that until he died. It was a common thing for visitors to come and have an audience with the lunatic.

Not only Truelock but several other inmates had a bible to hand and read the words—*behold, the devil shall cast some of you into prison… be thou faithful unto death, and I will give thee a crown for life.* Truelock made a habit of showing them the relevant passage.

The keepers of the asylum kept Truelock apart. A lunatic is easily swayed by scripture and could be roused by it and deranged by it—there are such parts of the bible—and would become an arm of Truelock's religion. With so many arms at hand, their keepers would no longer keep them.

The duties of the keepers at Bethlem are described as very arduous—the violent to restrain, the low and melancholy to cheer and cajole, the deluded to undeceive, the filthy to cleanse, the helpless to dress and undress and feed, and guide down the corridors, and to their plates and from their plates, and to their gruel and from their gruel, and to the yard and from the yard, all the while bearing the ill-tempers of many, and maintaining themselves in a state of persistent watchfulness, alarm, and anxiety.

Such as when Truelock told his fellows that the tongue is a two-edged sword, or may become one in the head of the Messiah, or the head of he who breathes the Messiah, by which he meant his own head as he stuck that head into the faces of his fellows with its tongue sticking out. Be mindful of my tongue, he told them, because it is a two-edged sword. This caused the inmates to come and look at his tongue, which was tough, and white, and scaled, and then inhale as Truelock exhaled, hoping to catch a waft of the Messiah and breathe him out themselves.

The relevant passage from Revelation is this—*And he had in his right hand seven stars: and out of his mouth went a sharp two-edged sword: and his countenance was as the sun shineth in his strength. And when I saw him, I fell at his feet as dead. And he laid his right hand upon me, saying unto me,* as Truelock said to his fellows, *Fear not: I am the first and the last: I am he that liveth, and was dead; and, behold, I am alive for evermore, Amen.*

And have the keys of hell and of death, he added, gesturing to the belt of the keeper and the keys that hung there, which Truelock, by his power of his thought, felt already between his fingers.

This habit of telling other inmates that the truest tongue has two sharp sides, and that it will tell the first and the last with words that cut the ears if they hear it, persisted well beyond Truelock's first telling. It became Bethlem lore and was still said when Jonathan arrived, along with stories of Truelock, and Hadfield, and other notable inmates, such as Patrick Walsh, who himself had killed a good few in there, was a ferocious maniac, wild as an animal, and surely, easily, passed the wild animal test.

Walsh enjoyed his sleep because he dreamt so well of killing his neighbours and would gleefully report how many souls he tore from their bodies that night. After a good night of vengeance, Walsh woke well pleased with himself, telling how he cut their throats and then walked around to see which would live longest, and that when they were all dead, or nearly so, he split open their heads and transposed their brains. Walsh put Hallwood's head into that of Lloyd, and Lloyd's brain into the head of Coates, and his to Jenkins, and then his to the skull of the poor Greek—to Walsh, he was always *that lousy Spaniard*—and then, when this was done, he switched their entrails, hung and burned them all, and was so very content with it until he entered the breakfasting hall the next morning and saw them sitting there, filling their mouths, alive, and not at all mixed up.

Walsh was able, at other times, to pretend contrition for his evil thoughts and his evil doings, which he did to obtain his snuff, of which he was passionately fond.

So, Hadfield, the would-be regicide, was not that bad at all. Even if he did do some bad at Bethlem, it was nothing in the shade of Walsh.

In addition to the head injuries, Hadfield also had his arm broken by a musket ball, the author notes, and in so doing the author squeezes a little more pleasure, or at least, a little more literary affect, from Hadfield's pain.

The regicide cast his own slugs from lead. The King was stood in his box at the Drury Lane Theatre and bowed with his usual condescension. The slug hit the roof of the box and the King kept on with his bowing and his condescension, so it was said.

During his stay at Bethlem, Hadfield had more luck in the activity of killing, striking a fellow maniac over the head, and Benjamin Swain, as he was called, died instantly. This was still nothing alongside Walsh.

Hadfield was assisted in his killing by the arrangement of furniture in the hall. Benjamin Swain fell after he was struck, caught over a bench behind him, with some speculating that the strike was feeble, but the subsequent fall was hard.

Otherwise, Hadfield was busy making straw baskets. He was permitted to sell these baskets, the Hadfield basket, as he called them, and his visitors would buy them for between six and eight shillings apiece, and take them home, and show them around, and say, look, a Hadfield basket, a souvenir from the would-be regicide, the King killer, who now sits in his cell and plays with straw. He subsisted on this basket income and his small military pension, and the provisions of his incarceration, of course.

The uneducated are naturally gifted for prophecy. Their minds operate more freely for want of instruction. They give prophecy as they receive it, with due credulity—one of the many charges against them.

Hadfield, who worked as a silversmith, is described as a vulgar, low-bred fellow, cleanly in his person, regular in his habits, knacky and ingenious in his amusements.

Truelock, the shoemaker, the prophet, also cleanly in his habits, declared the Bible a vulgar and indecent history with not a single sound argument inside it, least of all the New Testament, which is a series of falsehoods and absurdities.

Only an uneducated man could reject the Bible in this way, in its entirety, an uneducated man and a lunatic, who then offers his own prophecy in its place, a kind of presumptuous idiocy as the educated might call it, for which he has written seventy-eight signs, or so he says, although many of these signs are repetitions, and thereby fewer than the said total, but then many of those repetitions are accompanied by abundant remarks and comments, and so the assembled signs are likely more than the stated total of seventy-eight.

Truelock's signs would easily exceed that total of seventy-eight if these extra remarks were added on, which they might have been if Truelock's religion had taken hold, which it didn't. Of the signs that are repetitions, it is true that some of these are not exact repetitions but appear inverted or twisted, the whole assemblage being a medley of nonsense, and a sign, in itself, that Truelock was not capable of pronouncing judgement on anyone or anything, least of all himself.

The shoemaker was by all accounts also a very bad orthographer. It was near impossible to English his script.

He absconded only once and was found haggling with a bookseller whose services he could not afford, even if, as he persistently explained, the bookseller would never reap the rewards of his fee for publishing Truelock's doctrines and so should really do it for a littler amount, if not for nothing, since the world was ending, and Truelock was with child, the Messiah, and was about to exhale the contents of his belly.

This has to be the most exacting plea submitted by an author in recorded history. No publisher has been inveigled upon as this bookseller was by Truelock.

According to a different version of the story, Truelock left the bookseller and was only captured the following morning, after having spent the night in very un-prophetlike company.

That night the Messiah migrated downward, they joked.

Some of these details come from *Sketches in Bedlam*, published in 1823. It is signed by *A Constant Observer*, the author choosing to remain anonymous for what amounts to a 312 page-long slab of propaganda, the last 20 of which contain *Recommendary Attestations, selected, from several hundred inserted in the visitor book.*

A long list of Dukes, Duchesses, Earls, Lords, Barons, the odd Marquis, a foreign Prince, Directors, Doctors of Medicine, several Surgeons, a Governor and three Members of Parliament, various military officers and officials, though not a single priest, bishop, or archbishop, but then various others, mostly men, known only by their untitled selves, all come to visit this house of the insane and the criminally insane. They each manage to testify to the great cleanliness, attention, and order of the establishment and are more or less flatulent in their praise. Similar phrases are clustered together across separate entries as if visitors looked just above their own line for inspiration.

I have in no part of the world ever seen any hospital or establishment that compares to it in any way, one writes.

I have been struck with the highest admiration on viewing this establishment, as being more perfect than I could have considered possible, writes a second.

Should I ever be so unfortunate, writes a third, *as to render it necessary to be placed under restraint, I hope and trust my friends would select this place.*

He that hath an ear, let him hear—so the line begins in Revelation. The visitor book functions as an accumulation of ears, the author thinks, with each ear modelled on the one before it. But there must be an ear for that too, and for everything else that might be discovered about Bethlem, or Bedlam as it was more commonly known, a total institution about which only a total understanding will render Jonathan's stay there complete. A complete rendering of its architecture will be necessary, and its interiors too, that is to say all furnishings added after it was built, and then rebuilt, including the two statues in the main hall representing melancholic and raving madness each—these were removed by Jonathan's arrival, but older memories had them in place. And then the daily rituals of the place, when they were awoken, what they did, and when and how they were finally put to bed, and of what the beds were made, and how many of these beds were infested, and with what, and who worked there to clean it up and drive out pests, and who resided as inmates and as keepers, the particulars of every prisoner and lunatic before Jonathan, and a complete description of every character he met and did not meet but who lived there too during his own incarceration, and what they said, and how what they said formed the atmosphere, the lore, as the author describes it, of the institution. Its cracks must be rendered too, for these would have been studied by the bored, or by the curious, including those chained to their beds and those who woke at first light and those who lay in the yard and those that did not but stood and so between them surveyed different levels of movement that all buildings—even the best of them—must suffer after their construction.

What thou seest, write in a book, Revelation commands, *and I will give unto every one of you according to your works.*

6

Patrick Walsh would pick up pieces of glass, old nails, bones, and spoons wherever he could find them and conceal these objects about his person for subsequent grinding into points. These weapons were not all confiscated, and some were still in use, or in hiding, during Jonathan's time. Another detail, the author thinks, that cannot be set aside without cost.

Jonathan used one of these pointed spoons to carve out pictures and symbols in skirting boards, and doors, and under tables and benches. Many of these involved the son of Napoleon Bonaparte rising up from the sea to wipe England clean off the earth.

Incidentally, Walsh fought at Trafalgar and was stationed not far at all from the immortal Nelson.

The same image can be found in the frontispiece to *The Life of Jonathan Martin, Written by Himself*. Here it is executed rather better than the various marks he left about Bethlem since Jonathan had proper etching equipment to hand rather than the spoon. Or his brother William did it.

Walsh had sharpened the spoon for stabbing. Had he sharpened it for the purposes of the finer arts, Jonathan may have accomplished finer work in Bethlem.

Jonathan was also working at speed. This influenced his style and produced etched sons of Napoleon that were often missing complete limbs, or heads, or were oddly shaped.

In the second and the third editions of *The Life of Jonathan Martin*, a giant stands astride two harbour harms, one arm raised and holding a flaming torch, the other an arrow. In each edition, the giant has a halo of the prickling sort.

By the third edition, the giant had swapped over the arrow and the flaming torch so that one is in the left hand and the other in the right. The giant, who is otherwise naked, has also exchanged a fig-leaf ornament, or codpiece, from the second edition for some kind of skirt, or chastity belt, for the third. The inscriptions vary a little too.

Oh England prepare to meet thy God whilst thy Lamp yet holds out, runs the inscription in the second edition. Further down by the arrow the inscription goes on by suggesting that this same England better prepare *before Death like a piercing Dart goes forth.*

Hear Oh! England prepare to meet they God, runs the text in the third edition, *while thy lamp holds out to burn and before death like a piercing dart go forth.*

But anyone comparing the images side-by side will probably not focus on the differences in text, but on the odd codpiece to skirt transition, this and the fact that in the second edition there is also a ship beneath the giant, the mast of which points up to and very closely approaches the giant's rear.

Jonathan was probably working from an image he had seen or had in his possession of the fabled *Colossus of Rhodes*, which stood, by some accounts, astride the harbour and was numbered one of the Seven Wonders of the World. Engineers have declared that impossible, which would mean that no actual ships passed below the sun god's nether regions.

Walsh may well have preferred the second edition with the codpiece, although he did not have the opportunity to buy one being long enchained before Jonathan started hawking it about the place.

If Walsh had possessed the second edition and was told of what happened to the Colossus, he might have been breaking his inmates at the knee rather than switching their heads, or breaking them at the knee first, as preparation.

The Colossus lay for some eight centuries after it was broken at the knee by an earthquake.

The dream Walsh had in which he substituted Hallwood's brain for that of Lloyd, and Lloyd's brain for Coates, and so on, after which he switched their internal organs between them too, and set about the burning of it all, was really nothing much alongside all the torments of the Book of Revelation.

Such as when the fifth angel trumpeted and a bottomless pit opened from which poured enough smoke to darken the skies.

It bellowed locusts too with the power to sting as have scorpions on earth. They were not to kill but torment with their stings for the space of five months so that all men without the seal of God upon their foreheads will seek death and shall not find it. They shall desire their end but will find it flees before them and drags out their lives. These locusts will be like horses prepared for battle, with iron breastplates and wings that burst and make ears bleed with their noise. Each will bear a crown and come down upon their prey with faces as the faces of men, hair as the hair of women, and teeth as the teeth of the great cats. So, yes, what Walsh imagined was really nothing at all.

The first angel had already showered hail and fire mingled with blood and burnt up all grass and a third of all trees. And when the second angel trumpeted, a mountain burning with fire was cast into the sea and a third part of the sea became blood and a third part of its creatures perished and the same proportion—a third again—of all ships, destroyed, this angel again having a special liking of thirds, rather than quarters or halves.

The third angel had no such liking. It was left to the fourth to afflict again doom by the same amount, blackening a third part of the sun, a third of the moon, and a third of the stars, which took a third out of the day itself by some other miracle of celestial mechanics.

The sixth angel set about slaying the third part of all men remaining. This angel deployed horsemen on creatures with heads as lions, these breathed fire and smoke, and had tails as serpents, these smaller heads doing much hurt themselves.

Even before this destruction, all kings, and great men, and rich men, and captains, and mighty men, and free men, and so on down the long and dreary list of men-types, had lain before the mountains and rocks and said to those stones and piles of stones—*Fall on us, for we see that the great day of wrath is come, and who shall be able to stand?*

Jonathan had this passage in his head when he posted the letter on the gates of the Minster with the line, *will not the Greet, the mitey, the Rich men of the Earrth have to Call to the rocks and the hills to cover them From a Just and Angry Frauning God—*

This was the last repentance. All the work of the first six angels had got out of them all the repenting those men were capable of doing. Expended like that, no man was able to repent anymore during the destructions that the angels were planning—a somewhat crafty arrangement it has to be said. With no repenting left there would be no forgiveness or hope of forgiveness.

When Jonathan looked about him, he was sure to see that from the list of men-types, the most notable of them—the richest and most apparently holy—seemed least likely to do as was written in Revelation. They would not lay themselves before the next best thing in a country without mountains, namely their own churches and their cathedrals, and shout as they lay to the walls, towers, pillars, and arches, and the gargoyles, *Fall on us because our day has come.*

Gargoyles do occasionally kill by falling off, that is a sorry fact—and are not called down by their victims, which is even worse.

Lesser men tricked Jonathan into joining the navy, but Jonathan saved a good part of his ire for the better men, the beef eaters, card players, and hypocrites. It was common enough to despise the priesthood, given how the established church had made so much profit and grown so fat from the land enclosures of the previous century, each enclosure an excuse to double the tithe, their tax, and further immiserate the poor. As the priests left their thatch cottages, built country estates, and joined the gentry, cottagers were forced to give up their livestock and way of living for the workhouse.

One way of defending the priesthood was to argue that the validity of the ordinance did not depend on the piety or even the morality of the minister. But it was a feeble defence, at the time.

Jonathan was gazing at the Monument in London when they got him, telling him there was a nicely paid job in the merchant navy rather than a poorly paid job in His Majesty's Killing Fleet.

The Monument commemorates the great fire of 1666, and Jonathan had just finished having read to him—and translated—the line blaming the pope for his hand in it.

Sed Furor Papisticus Qui Tamdiu Patravit Nondum Restingvitur.

This was chiselled off in 1830. Jonathan next inspected the north side in which is written how many days it raged, how many buildings it destroyed—89 churches, 13,200 houses, 400 streets, many gates, edifices, libraries, hospitals, and schools—and how much was left mutilated and half burned, and how far the ashes extended, and how merciless were the flames, and swift and rowdy was the burning, *and how it reminded us of the final destruction of the world by fire.* The man who read and translated the inscriptions for him said that the monument was built on the foundation of the first church lost to the blaze, one of the few churches not rebuilt, replaced instead by this finger of stone.

Jonathan gave a false name when he was enlisted. That was a sensible first mutiny. If Jonathan was not known under his true name, they would not so easily retrieve him once he fled. The boatswain took one look, and the man with a false name became a foretopman, which meant he was assigned to the masts at the foretop, if that makes any sense.

This first assignment, the *Hercules*, was a 74-gun, third-rate ship. It was stolen from the French and used by the British to return its destructions.

Fairly soon, he acquired the basics of ropes and rigging. This knowledge would come in useful. Jonathan made it out of York Minster by using the bell rope, which he cut down, set with knots, and slung from the window. These knots were definite evidence that a mariner had done it, said those who saw the thing.

His approach was basic and effective. Jonathan asked his fellow seamen the names of various ropes and followed where they led to. By that naming and that following, he became acquainted with their function. He also learned how to run aloft, and climb, and swing over and under, and tug, and knot, and so on, and sleep and eat in his confined quarters, and develop his sea legs, as they called them because the first thing a new seaman does is learn afresh how to walk.

In 1807, they did some killing at Copenhagen, and capturing, and delivering of troops. Sailors were landed to erect batteries, and they fired rockets on a church that the Danes then attempted to save. Many of them died attempting that. Jonathan watched it go, the church and the Danes about it, when the rest of the seamen onboard were watching one of their own, a small ship, run aground and destroyed by retort. He saw the flames travel up the spire and form a column, and eventually a line of smoke, not unlike the pillar of fire and the pillar of cloud that guided Moses through the desert, he thought, this Moses who was a murderer, as his brother later said, a man who took all the negativity from the word and left only the positive.

When Jonathan was a little boy, his older brother Richard the Quartermaster-Sergeant, told him that he could make ants pop by firing at them with the sun. This by the aid of a lens. He thought about that when he saw the Danes rushing about the church.

The Danes flew a flag of truce and begged two days to bury their dead, which was granted, and then a further four days, which was refused. Surrender entirely or we will reduce your city to ashes, they were told, and Jonathan listened to that too.

The English spent the next seven weeks emptying the dockyards of all their stores. Jonathan recalls that for all seven weeks not three in 24 hours were allowed for rest, there being so much plunder to collect.

Their great sin was to dance on deck each Sunday, as invited by the Captain. Jonathan joined in for fear of giving offence. The ship was later caught in a hurricane. The waters burst the lower deck gun ports, the sea occupied the ship. Men swam between decks, and everything that could float did so, including mess tables, and barrels, and crates. It pleased god to pity us, Jonathan later recalled, but the giving of pity is not the same as the granting of absolution, of which there was none.

After the *Hercules*, Jonathan was moved to an 84-gun ship, with seven others, to blockade some Russian ships at Lisbon.

Then, in 1809, some time was spent off Corunna, watching the bloated carcases of horses as they floated down the river and into the sea. Soon after that, they watched the English and French armies blasting one another from their hilltop positions before those English soldiers who survived this last battle of their overland retreat fled to the transport ships, which were then blasted too. During all that bombardment from their pitiless attackers, several transports were sunk, the sea doing its own job too in the sinking. The remaining ships fled with their bloodied cargo, including men who had been both injured on land and then all but drowned at sea, with the lot of them occupying the cockpit, cable tier, and every other spare place on board each ship, with their moans and their dying and their variously expressed fears of dying—it was a narrow repertoire, Jonathan thought, the sound of human pain. This went on for some time and gave much opportunity to listen, for the wounded could not be helped due to the tempest which followed and kept all able seamen busy. The wounded who could grip held on. Those who could not rolled and knocked against each other and against those who did still retain their purchase. Five more transports were lost before they reached Plymouth, and scores lay dead on those boats that did arrive. Jonathan had accumulated a fair bit of doomsday material to work with, by this point. Enough to enliven the dreams of the least susceptible, the author suspects.

A few days after, and with the decks scrubbed free of the recent suffering, they left for Lisbon. Jonathan had now served on the foretop, forecastle, gunner's crew, and afterguard, and was made captain of the foretop on a fresh ship stolen from the Spanish. He was also employed as a signal man in a gunboat, and captain of a main deck gun, as well as a boarder, a fireman, and a mortar boatman. His itinerancy on board can only be explained by the number of crew, in all these positions, who died, or fell sick, or fell overboard, or absconded each time the ship made port. Either that or nobody could stand him, and each found an excuse for moving him on. Jonathan was still piping on about the dancing they did after the siege of Copenhagen and made a habit of spotting other similar cycles of sin and divine retribution. He was inundated with examples of each.

7

During their sailing to Cadiz, the gunner's yeoman shot himself dead. This was hardly worth remembering—suicide onboard was not uncommon—but what made Jonathan tell of it was where it was done, in the storeroom, about which more than 500 barrels of gunpowder were stacked. He had the good wit with several others to go down and put out the fire that the wadding had made. It was only a small fire, he recalled. But the sound of the pistol and their knowing of the place of its firing caused some amount of leaping overboard until it became apparent that the ship would not explode, and only the mess of the yeoman's head would have to be faced, which it was, with the usual perfunctory clean-up.

Jonathan saved 600 men that day, so he said.

—so did the yeoman, said some of the crew, for having fired the pistol up, and not across, or down.

When Jonathan tried to do what his brother Richard had told him with the ants, he failed. These ants did not seem to be the popping kind. At best they crumpled below the rays he accumulated to a point. Most just ran a bit faster. He asked Richard to show him, but the future Quartermaster-Sergeant said that he had other things to invent and that ant popping was now behind him. In this respect Richard followed his older brother William, *The Philosophical Conqueror of All Nations*, who took his childhood inventing into his adulthood and went on with it from one great innovation to the next. Ant popping was soon beneath him too.

Their brother John, the future artist, also got into the habit of solving all material problems, or at least thinking about solving them, such as his plan to improve the London sewage system—a side effect of which would be a better water supply for pointing at fires, among other things. This obsessed him for years.

After the trial and committal of his brother, John gave up his painting for his sewage treatment scheming. Somehow, painting vast scenes of biblical destruction didn't entertain him as it had, now that Jonathan had so very publicly exceeded him in material effect.

It was only an intermission. John, the artist, returned to his painting of scenes of wrath, destruction, and judgement. This included a smaller one called *Pandemonium*. He did that after Jonathan died in Bethlem. This painting, of modest proportions but extraordinary violence, has the earth erupt fire and lava in the foreground. It does that before a building that exceeds the cathedral at York tenfold, and so it would burn tenfold too.

When most of the seamen were breakfasting down below, Jonathan escaped the man of war on which he was kept. A small group of friends, or a group of some sort, perhaps they wished him gone, formed a circle at the forecastle. He was then lowered onto a boat brought there for that purpose. The ex-foretopman rowed to the waterman's house, in which Jonathan stayed until the ship had sailed. It is not clear what port this was, but from that place, Jonathan managed to get work on a transport bound for Egypt. It was to collect corn for our troops, as he said. These troops were then lying at Messina, in Sicily, a city that had been and would again be destroyed by earthquakes.

Newly arrived in Egypt, Jonathan roved about seeing not the Egypt of the nineteenth century—the place with the corn to deliver for the English troops—but the Egypt of the Old Testament, in which Joseph stores huge quantities of grain, so much grain he gave up recording it, for it was beyond measure.

Joseph made a killing, one might say, in the next seven years of famine, selling the stuff to the inhabitants of that country, and those of other countries too.

Some Turks, as Jonathan said, even took him to see all the different buildings that the corn was stored in, back then, several thousand years earlier as the Old Testament has it.

Because Joseph had stored so much of it, the tour took some time, and expense. There were so many old ruins and not so old ruins to see.

Jonathan also kept half an eye for the seven ugly cows eating the seven fat cows, but only saw ugly cows looking for fodder. He knew this was deluded, his looking for the cows, but he did it anyway.

The young Jonathan did also try fire, too, with the ants. He used the stem of dried-out corn—which is what the British call wheat—as a splint, and held the fire next to the ants to see if that would make them pop. This second experiment gave the same result as the first. Faster running, or stationary and crumpled. It was at this point that Jonathan stopped with the ants.

In Egypt, Jonathan observed one of those idiotic scuffles that sometimes occurs between men. It involved some camel drivers and the crew of another transport ship. The camel drivers were resting when the crew came ashore in a small boat seeking fresh water, and one of those sitting with the camels took a fancy to the captain's spy glass, which he attempted to snatch and which was resisted, during which the captain was stabbed, and the rest of them fled. I was roving about nearby, Jonathan said, and had just approached the camels to see what they were laden with when it all began. Thinking Jonathan was one of the crew, they set on them too, until one interceded and had the dagger withdrawn. It was Abraham's God that did it and prevented his death, his certain death, as Jonathan felt it at the time. This was one of many examples of his deliverance.

His providential escape from a watery grave would be another example of deliverance. And the three escapes which occurred after that too, Jonathan being a frequent faller into the water.

There is a woodcut in the second edition of the *Life of Jonathan Martin,* and then another in the third, depicting the different stages of falling in from the very top of the ship—this happens just as waves near engulf it—and the different stages of being hauled out so that he could climb to the top and fall back in again.

One of these Jonathan figures in the woodcut is so engulfed by the waters that only his feet can be seen, by which it can be assumed he fell head first.

The waves are executed in the woodcut by parallel lines. These each end with a curl, the whole of it supposed to resemble a fearful inundation of water, but looking, the author feels, more like human hair or a wig, in which the ship has become entangled.

I fell from the main yard, Jonathan writes. That is, he fell from one of those horizontal beams, or spars, from which the sails are hung. I was there on the end and then found myself falling, finding, as I did so, a bit of rope, from which he ended dangling, arms taut, their pits drawn flat. I was just above the sea, he said. Just a few feet, waiting for his shipmates, his face inflamed and raised up by the jowls. They set to, sticking poles out, none of which was long enough, until the ship rolled and yawed him close to grab.

His next fall was from lower down. Somehow, Jonathan managed this one out of a gun port.

And then he fell from the topgallant yard, which is one of the highest horizontals. The topping lift broke, he went down, grappled with the backstay, and landed on the cross trees. None of which makes any sense to most people.

Otherwise put, Jonathan fell from near the top, because something broke, but did not manage to fall the entire 80 feet, which would have killed him.

Another reason to praise Almighty. Here in the second edition, and also in the third, Jonathan declares he will not trespass on the patience of his readers any further, but be assured, there were plentiful other examples of a similar nature.

Jonathan, it seems, received one deliverance after the next, year on year, until he finally escaped the whole hellish business of not dying at sea.

Which meant the Almighty could take a break from all the deliverances.

Which must have been something too.

This was the time of Jonathan's second desertion at the mouth of the Tagus. The sailor was set on shore with a number of others to procure the brushwood used to scour the decks. With the prospect of much bending and scouring ahead, Jonathan sought his opportunity.

Go get some twigs, the midshipman told his party, walking himself, very decisively, to a wine house. Once in the woods, and with the midshipman probably well tanked already, Jonathan and his shipmate left the gathering of sticks and walked themselves—in their own decisive way—as far from their duties as they could, so that their duties could become memories, and these memories fade, and another life, of some sort—they had not really pictured it—would replace the one that was fading, with all the falls, and the deliverances, and the scrubbing, and the various other jobs, the multiple daily and nightly duties, the chafing observances that a sailor must attend to and that nobody else will ever truly picture.

The two English sailors reached the river where the ferryman saw and indeed heard them, long before they, looking up, saw him. There he was, standing, entirely silent and watchful. The man knew what they were about and refused them passage. English sailors were not particularly welcome in this part of the world. His Majesty's Killing Fleet did have something to do with it—the sailors always landed with such appetites.

This was nothing against the English, specifically. The French and Spanish were awful too.

These are all of them considerable understatements. Even overstatements would be understatements, the author feels.

Some kind of threat was made against the ferryman—of his life, of his livelihood, it is not clear which—and they made it over the river on the ferry they commandeered, and then on, and further, and finally to a different wine-house where they felt, really, deservedly, they might take a little refreshment.

They left the place intoxicated, very pleased, most likely, with this new life of domination. They would easily domineer and cajole all these inland waterways, so it seemed, and take its ferries whichever way they felt, and drink, and drink, and never see another deck or another fistful of brushwood.

A land eviscerated by war can be a happy place to roam.

This was the occasion when Jonathan—after more journeying of a kind—finally came to his senses and looking down at his legs found himself without trousers. Perhaps they had been exchanged for wine, he could think of no other explanation.

And he started to walk like a man without trousers, which he had not yet done, roving instead, till then, like a man who has had a bellyful of wine, which looks different.

He asked the Portuguese woodsman they met next for direction, again like a man might do when not wearing any trousers—and so not at all like a man would ask with them on. This may well have influenced the exchange, that and their near complete ignorance of the language.

Unbearable thirst and hunger passed between them, with each shipmate telling the awfulness of their feeling of it until there was no energy left for that, and they both lay down for a while, one deciding to drop and the other following until that laying down became irksome in its own way, and they dragged on, and up, and round hills, still not clear of the woods they first came to their senses in, after the drinking, and the ferry—the commandeering of which was no longer such a noble memory, and not even a fond one. In that state, they did not even remember their fonder memories with pleasure or regard anything at all in their existence in a positive way.

On the second morning, they came across five houses, all victims of bombardment, so they thought, not being well acquainted with the rural poverty and dilapidation of these parts and the general decline that is the consequence of protracted war. The French army must be near and be the cause of it, they decided, and so fled as fast as half-starved, dehydrated men could flee. But then, a little further, came upon the coast, and it was Lisbon, and it was their ship, just there, still at anchor.

It was surely death by hanging, yet before that definite prospect there might be a little drink, they thought, and perhaps some food, so they grovelled their way back on board and begged and told as much of the truth as they could, the bit about getting drunk, and being lost, and not the bit about deserting. Looking very much like recent drunkards do, they were pardoned and taken back to the work of the ship.

The next time Jonathan made landfall in Lisbon, on a different ship, during a different visit, they were delivering English soldiers to engage the French. He did a better job of making off and succeeded in fleeing in a straight line rather than a circle.

Along the way he taught the Portuguese peasants how better to reap their harvest. He knew to hold a sickle, so he told them, and made a sheaf with two cuts what took them forty.

An old man came running over, crying *BONE, STAR BONE*. Its meaning in English is *John Engly that is well done,* as Jonathan interpreted, now knowing more Portuguese than he did previously. He was presented with a purse of Spanish dollars for his well-cut sheaf, and for the lesson of it, and simply for the pleasure of having a good Englishman about the place.

The old man took me home with him and gave me plenty of the best cheer, showing me his land, which was good, and his house, which was commodious, and a young lady, who looked the part, and she cried out *BONE, STAR BONE, JOHN ENGLY, FOR YU RESTAY,* its meaning in English being, *If you will stay we will do you good.* It was clear to him that here he might settle and marry and listen to them speak such excellent Portuguese. But they worshipped wooden gods, he came to realise, and when they spoke to him, these wooden gods cracked open their mouths and spoke too and infested all wooden objects.

Once more, Jonathan returned to his ship, retracing his straight line inland back to sea. The ship was at anchor, and the wine houses nearby nearly dry, and he had not yet been missed.

He went below deck and inspected his hands, and his feet, and the rest of the skin for any splinters from the wooden objects, since these might infest the ship, he judged, and he would be trapped at sea suffering again those gods which would crack open the grains of the wood, he was sure, and begin speaking to him from all sides. He found not a single splinter and praised his own god once again for his protection.

Assigned to a transport ship, Jonathan was next loading sulphur in Sicily, there being a volcano, hopefully extinct, that was full of the stuff. They procured asses to visit the mines, and his companions on their return, with the asses laden and the yellow rock reaching out from the pannier baskets, went in for some drinking, and cavorting, and insulting those they passed, including some Italians who did not take well to the five men on their asses. Jonathan was still carrying the memory of looking down at his legs and finding no trousers—an event that did, it seemed, make a disproportionate impact on his mind. He drank now in moderation and, from his comparatively sober vantage, noticed the Italians as they unfolded their knives—as Italians are wont to do—and prepared for their roadside murdering. Fleeing his ass to run among them and beg, Jonathan made such an impression of English fragility, or is it idiocy, that the Italians folded back their knives and relented.

This reminded Jonathan of another siege of Copenhagen detail, the mule he commandeered, when sent to do some foraging, the neck of which he subsequently slit because the Danes were near and the mule would not give up its braying. There was a daemon stuck in its throat, he decided. It would be a kindness to let it out.

The animals of that country seemed against him. Upon raiding a house that gave nothing up and turning instead to its apple tree about which he climbed, a mastiff came to the foot of it and growled and barked at the Englishman. Fortunately, he found a small bit of biscuit in his pocket. This appeased the mastiff and allowed his descent. Although the apples were abundant, and he now had a basket full, he could hear the voices of the Danes very distinctly and so left the tree and that excursion with no victuals at all for his crew.

Jonathan was by now familiar with his own self-reflection, tacking from one country to another and taking in the vastness of the oceans and its creatures and the wars which were at that time tracing lines across its surfaces. Jonathan saw how it spoke to him. The world itself addressed him from its reaches.

Which was nothing out of the ordinary. The world addresses many men in this way, all men, or those many men, who feel themselves in their pleasures and their suffering at its very centre. With Jonathan, however, the world communicated so that Jonathan was not only his own ripe spokesperson—the destiny of the majority—but spoke for that world too. Its magmas then materialised in his mind, as he might have said. Or as somebody else might venture. The thought of everything at once, this falling in of its vastness, hurt him in the head.

Sailing off Cadiz, a shipmate told him of the trick he knew, that bad things need stringing out, he said, rather like the fragments of this book, the author felt, which is the only way of seeing them each individually. No mind can handle, and no book can endure, all things occurring at once—so much to their detriment.

Actually, the least that should be done, the author feels, is to avoid those details amalgamating because they will not group together as Jonathan felt them but will be assembled, in this, a literary context, as a mood, or a style of delivery, that connects each detail to the next, presenting a fraudulent image, a continuous narrative, or an atmosphere within which all things are connected to all other things. There is too much harmony in a novel.

8

A total understanding of Jonathan's perception, a proper rendering of his totalising vision, will always be betrayed by the finality of writerly mechanics which at once disfigure the world and shield the book within the enclosed satisfactions of print.

Efforts to make that world of derangement enter the mechanics of writing always struck the author as futile, perhaps infantile. It was at times symptomatic of exterior derangement—which the author had time for—but more often bookish derangements are affected. No such book has broken its binding of its own accord by the force of the words within its pages. The glue still holds, the gutters are tight.

So many signs of pain and the intolerable burden of living, Jonathan felt, as he himself could not assemble in his consciousness, but which he felt in the weight of his thinking.

Bethlem, for instance, was intolerably short of toilets, even in the newly designed building, with one toilet, one sink, and one cold bath at the end of each gallery. They put the incontinent patients to bed on straw.

Meanwhile, visitors kept returning and reporting on the amusing objects they were met with, the many excellent stories they were told, and the mad frolics they witnessed.

His last deliverance at sea occurred in the voyage home from Sicily, the final trip which occurred before this man, who had aged some since he was press-ganged, was finally paid off from the transport service.

The cargo of sulphur previously mentioned was below, and the ship was well on its way, and its crew well exhausted so that only four men could be roused for the night watch, Jonathan included. Looking windward, he saw a tremendous wave, a grotesque upheaval in the ocean, hardly space to shout to the helm to *ease off* before this wave took about them.

When lesser waves approach, all who can will grasp the taffrail as their best support, but Jonathan managed only to get hold of the iron stanchion below it. This was again the work of providence. As the wave struck, it tore the taffrail from the ship, carrying too the bulwarks and every movable on deck. Even the bolts which secured the arm-chest were torn from their purchases. Their cargo shifted and the beams fell level with the wash of its turning over. All hands below deck and Jonathan too went to secure what they could, driving cleats into the deck to coil their cables on. Many cried that the ship was going down, for it was still on its beam ends. On his knees at last, Jonathan felt his own futility before the great unanswerable, having only pushed himself that far already with the firmness of despair.

All so very good and convincing, the author feels, because the author knows nothing of such things and had to look up words like *cleat* and *taffrail* and know to write *arm-chest* and not *arms-chest*—words taken with so many other phrases from Jonathan's own writing, here and elsewhere, and with them the air of situated knowledge, then warped and repurposed. Carriers still of the effect of knowing what is being talked about.

The only consolation in the author's ignorance being that of perpetuating it.

As the author knows well, this writing renders it difficult, and in some cases impossible, to determine which details are plagiarised and which are improvised by linguistic association and associative composition. The author, too, begins to forget.

The author works towards a point of exhaustion where caring for the veracity of words, where attempts to police the division between fiction and fact, break off. Which is not the same as confusing fiction with actuality. The terms are themselves abandoned.

The ship did eventually answer the helm, and the captain was heard shouting it so, and twelve hours later the whole was upright, and, with the help of God, as many of them declared, they got safe to Portsmouth in a few days. It was 1810.

Another eighteen years would have to elapse before the firing of York Minster, which meant another eighteen years of its organ sounding and its dignitaries and choirs sitting in the north and south stalls of the chancel, folding up and folding down the miserere, or mercy-seats.

Which is probably the place to mention how the miserere, or mercy-seat, can be leant upon when the seat is up—it wraps around a little, so helping its occupant to endure long and arduous church services.

When Jonathan was finished, only the ordinary benches of the nave were left unburnt, where there was no such provision, and standing must be endured without assistance.

It would be another eighteen years of the more occasional ensconcing of the archbishop's throne, too, and of the daily climbing to the pulpit—also fired—and, of course, the existence of the fourteenth-century roof—a marvel by all accounts—and all the lead which would drip to the floor. Jonathan had much dreaming and roving to endure before all that was done and obliterated, and he would be incarcerated too, for a while, in a small northern asylum.

The reader does not have to endure as much of it as Jonathan did since not so much is known of his wandering years.

Actually, the reader will always endure much less of everything. The reader is a gnat, not even an afterthought.

This was the period of Jonathan's fall into prophecy, of his apparent and growing lunacy. But the lunacy of his prophecy appears less and less crazed, the author feels, the more the author inspects the man's contemporaries.

His was merely one commentary in a range of dissenting and increasingly common lexicons of complaint. These were the years of invention, of repurposing words, by which the rottenness of society was diagnosed.

Which is a lengthy way of saying Jonathan was merely one disordered visionary in a world of derangements.

Or that a world of derangements produces disordered vision—new points of dismemberment.

And that his own personal disorder was less dangerous than the call to order which answered it. Until, that is, he did his mischief.

Although nobody died at York Minster when it was burning.

Even if they did, for Jonathan the call to order, which is really a call to do nothing before catastrophe, is worse.

It was too ordinary a thing to prophesy the end—they were all doing that—but still far too occasional to enact it.

The problem is that the end of things tends to arrive piecemeal, which is why almost nobody notices it happen, or if they do, almost nobody is convulsed by the prospect.

To which must be added that for each radical millenarian prophet, there was a township of weak interpreters. The language of millenarian thought was so commonplace almost anyone could speak it without transgressing their social ties. That language, that imagery would have to be wrenched from a context where the Antichrist could be brought up in conversation without causing unsettlement or a quickened pulse. Or the language of it would be abandoned altogether.

Jonathan's lunacy may simply be the consequence of his *antinomian* outlook, the author writes. He was released by divine grace from the norms of established thinking and established morality. Jonathan was not obliged to observe the law or fear the judgement of people who are formed by it, who cannot imagine how anyone could live in excess of it.

Which would allow him to set fire to cathedrals, for instance, and look upon himself on trial as a quirk, an oddity, standing there in bodily submission but nonetheless existing in excess of their enslavement to the nomos.

As Jonathan drew himself, or the son of Napoleon, so was his mission. It was time to strike at the stars and bring them down and trample them underfoot. He shall devour the earth, tread it over, and break it to pieces. And to anyone who complains at his destructions, and cries against them, and suggests that all is not so bad and that some of it should be protected, this giant will say, but look, how easily it crumples.

By divine grace, Jonathan Martin exceeded the reach of civilised thinking, the author wrote, and then came to think that these words were too civilised themselves and found the irony hard to bear.

Antinominalism is a specific term, a technical term for religious excess, and should not be confused with fanaticism, the author thinks, which is an open term that means almost nothing when applied to others.

Fanaticism, in its use, is one of those words that signals the end of thinking, a prohibition to think any further.

Religious fanaticism menaces annihilation of reason, common sense, and the science of the nation—these words appeared in *The Gentleman's Magazine* in May 1828 and were directed at fanatics in general, but they applied just as well to Jonathan Martin, his contemporaries would have thought.

Moral feelings, also, are annihilated by religious fanaticism. Social structure is threatened. Political order too. Everything is done in by so much religious enthusiasm, or at least by its perversion into *enthusiastical mysticisms*. So wrote Thomas Mortimer in *Die and be damned*.

This was the book being reviewed in *The Gentleman's Magazine*.

And all of these accusations may be true. They notice the threat of fanaticism but set their words against it in a gesture of absolute closure.

Mortimer's book was first published in 1758. The third edition, revised & enlarged, had a subtitle too, so that the whole read, *Die and be damned. Or, a policy of insurance against Methodism and enthusiasm*. This edition was printed in 1761.

By 1828 the subtitle was more tactful—*Die and be damned. Or a policy of insurance against Fanaticism*. That was the edition reviewed in *The Gentleman's Magazine*.

We have only to say, the reviewer writes, *that we have seen very few pamphlets which have the judgement, eloquence, and reason of this. It shows that modern fanaticism is entirely unchristian.*

The title, as Mortimer explains, is a subterfuge. It is designed to entice those who speak in such terms, who preach or like to hear men preach of eternal damnation, into reading Mortimer's book. Those who say *you must die and will be damned*, and take this as one of their favourite expressions in common conversation, would first pick up Mortimer's book—some might call it a pamphlet—because of that subterfuge. And, having now picked it up, will be persuaded by Mortimer's use of reason and Mortimer's irrefutable argument that they were duped into saying that—this thing about how you must die and be damned. They will understand that by saying it, they were conned into thinking it. That each time they said it, they thought it, and so they should leave off saying it. This was Mortimer's intelligent design.

What can account for all the quarrels and wars that have so disgraced Christian history, Mortimer wonders, or appears to wonder, because Mortimer has already concluded. As St. Peter has told us, he writes, *the unstable and the unlearned*. It is they who have done it. The unstable and the unlearned *wrest all scriptures to their destruction*. If the religious fanatic is not unstable, the fanatic is unlearned, and if the religious fanatic is not unlearned, the fanatic must be unstable. It is a simple enough formula.

Mortimer was largely self-taught. This allowed him to tell himself that he pretty much gave himself those elements of sound thinking and reasoned argument that he found lacking elsewhere, mainly among the lower orders of society.

His knowledge was chiefly due to his own efforts, as the entry has it in the *Dictionary of National Biography*, published in 1894.

This Mortimer bettered himself by studying elocution, among other things. All of which might explain his particular intolerance for the unlearned, which runs throughout *Die and be damned* as its most recurring accusation. The self-taught can have special contempt for those who have not made the effort. Their contempt is cultivated rather than bred.

But Mortimer's disdain was more focused than that. He did not despise the unlearned for their lack of education—it made no sense to do so since mass education had not yet been invented. Only those who rose from the mob to teach that mob fell accused. These teachers were the false prophets of his century.

The author came to like this formula for a while. If a person rose from the lower class, the mob, the rabble, and no longer submitted to their station, *at this moment, they became unlearned.* So long as they remained below, they could neither be learned nor unlearned. These categories would not apply. They had *vulgar minds*, which was different.

Two conclusions might be drawn from the switch in title from *a policy of insurance against Methodism and enthusiasm* to *a policy of insurance against Fanaticism*. First, that methodism was not worth upsetting too much, by 1828, and second, and relatedly, that methodism had begun to stabilise and become learned. It was growing organised, and mainstream, and gradually absorbed into the establishment. When Jonathan roved about in his wandering years, methodism was in the process of becoming respectable in this way. This placed him at its growing fringe.

Law destroyers are often profligate law creators, the author thinks, and can be tolerated as such for as long as all their own law-making is still disordered, and disorderly.

After his final landing at Portsmouth, I took to London, and then to Newcastle, Jonathan writes, to see my parents—the two of them would be dead soon—found employment in County Durham, got married, had a son, named him Richard.

This being when his mother came to tell Jonathan he would be hanged, or her ghost told him that, or his memory of her person, with her being dead of course.

His sister Ann was also there in this vision of the prophecy of his hanging. But all that has already been mentioned.

Ann was not yet dead and would outlive him too.

Ann does not appear in the *Dictionary of National Biography*, aside from the line *and there was one daughter*, in the entry for William Martin, her being his sister.

Richard does not appear in the *Dictionary of National Biography* either, not under his own name. But there are a couple of lines about Richard in William's segment, about his service in the Peninsular War, and that he was at Waterloo.

William, Jonathan, and John, who do appear in the dictionary under their own names, are separated out from one another by several other Williams, Jonathans, and Johns.

It is hard not to return to the predicted hanging, the author felt, and wonder how that influenced his trial. Jonathan was remarkably cheerful, by all accounts, and was only irked when he discovered that Richard had contrived a defence of lunacy, which would mean that he would not be executed after all.

So it was that Jonathan discovered he would not be hanged by the neck, and so on.

He found that out, about his mother being wrong, yet again as he took ill a decade after, lay his head back, and prepared to die.

He also discovered or came to realise, or should have realised had he thought about it, that his mother, or the ghost of his mother—or whatever mother thing came to him—was another one of those false prophets denounced for as long as the bible was written.

I had been preparing for years for my hanging, Jonathan said, and then it turned out I would not be hung. After all that preparatory work, this not being hung was harder to bear than it might sound, he might have added.

His mother had him by the umbilical. She had been yanking the cord for as long as he could breathe.

But living like that, with a cord, or the prophecy of a cord, is curiously releasing. If Jonathan knew that he would be hanged, he could no longer *risk* a capital offence. Which is to say, a capital offence—such as burning a cathedral or killing a bishop—is no longer a risk, as such, or not a terminal one. This, precisely, was the wisdom of his mother, or the mother thing that came to him in his dream.

The dream about being in a violent storm came next, and about it sounding like great guns resounding as he had heard them do.

And then the one about the redeemer appearing in the clouds, praying for him from that lofty position, which seemed promising.

Then was the parable of the barren fig tree, told to Jonathan in Jonathan-like words and with Jonathan intonations.

The Jonathan way of telling also told to himself of his sitting in a field, and of the great fire that came towards him, and then around him, and how he pondered from that encircled place if this was it, and if that was the world's end, and if he, who was at the centre of all things ending, would be eternally lost. By which he meant eternally unredeemed and not lost because there is no better way of being located than he was, here, there, at the epicentre of the end of everything that ever existed.

I was much disturbed, Jonathan said, and took to reading my bible as best as I could, which, from the little heed taken of my education, was not very well.

These last words are verbatim, the author wrote, wishing to be reminded of that in case it was forgotten.

JONATHAN MARTIN

THE LUNATIC,

Who set York Minster on Fire, February 2, 1829

From a Painting by Mr. E. Lindley, taken in Prison, by permission of t[he] Magistrates.

March 31, 1829.   YORK;—Published by H. BELLERBY, 13, Stonegate.

SECOND EDITION, CONSIDERABLY IMPROVED.

THE LIFE OF JONATHAN MARTIN,

OF DARLINGTON, TANNER.

Written by Himself.

CONTAINING

Account of the Extraordinary Interpositions of Divine Providence on behalf, during a period of six years' service in the Navy, including his wonderful escapes in the Action of Copenhagen, and in many affairs on the Coasts of Spain and Portugal, in Egypt, &c. Also, an Account of the Embarkation of the British Army after the Battle of Corunna. Likewise an Account of his subsequent Conversion and christian Experience, with the Persecutions he suffered for Conscience' sake, being locked up in an asylum and ironed, describing his miraculous Escape through the roof of the house, having first ground off his Fetters with a Sandy Stone. His singular Dream of the Destruction of London, and the Host of Armed Men overrunning England, &c. &c.

Barnard-Castle:
PRINTED FOR AND SOLD BY THE AUTHOR, BY THOMAS CLIFTON

1826.

Price Eight Pence.

Jonathan Martin's Providential Escape from a Watery grave in the Bay of Biscay, at different times:

Jonathan Martin's Providential Escape from the Asylum House.

Hear Oh! England prepare to meet thy God, while thy Lamp holds to burn and before death like a a piercing dart go forth.

WHEREAS
JONATHAN MARTIN

Stands Charged with having on the Night of the 1st of February, Instant,

WILFULLY SET FIRE TO

YORK MINSTER.

A REWARD OF
100 *POUNDS*

Will be Paid on his being Apprehended and Lodged in any of his Majesty's Gaols.

And a Further Reward of

One Hundred Pounds

Will be paid on the Conviction of any ACCOMPLICES of the said JONATHAN MARTIN, to such Person or Persons as shall give Information which may lead to such Conviction.

The following is a Description of the said Jonathan Martin: viz.

He is rather a Stout Man, about Five Feet Six Inches high, with light Hair cut close, coming to a point in the centre of the Forehead, and high above the Temples, and has large bushy Red Whiskers; he is between Forty and Fifty Years of Age, and of singular Manners. He usually wears a single-breasted blue Coat, with a stand-up Collar, and Buttons covered with the same cloth; a black cloth Waistcoat; and blue cloth Trowsers; Half-Boots laced-up in front; and a glazed, broad-brimmed, low-crowned Hat. Sometimes he wears a double-breasted blue Coat with yellow Buttons.—When Travelling, he wears a large black leather Cape coming down to his Elbows, with two Pockets within the Cape; there is a square piece of dark coloured Fur, extending from one shoulder point to the other.—At other times he wears a drab coloured great Coat, with a large Cape and shortish Skirts.—When seen at York last Monday, he had on the double-breasted blue coat, a common Hat, and his great Cost.

The said JONATHAN MARTIN is a Hawker of a Pamphlet entitled "The Life of Jonathan Martin, of Darlington, Tanner," the Third Edition of which is printed at Lincoln, by R. E. LEARY, 1828.—He had lodged in York about a Month, and quitted it on the 27th of January last, stating that he was going to Tadcaster for a few Days, and thence to Leeds. He returned to York on the 31st of January, and said that he and his Wife had taken Lodgings in Leeds. He was not seen in York after the 1st of February.

By Order of the DEAN and CHAPTER of YORK,
CHRIST. JNO. NEWSTEAD,
Clerk of the Peace for the Liberty of St. Peter of York.

York, 5th February, 1829.

BARNES & CO. PRINTERS, NORTH SHIELDS.

MARTIN
Apprehended.

Jonathan Martin,

Who stands charged with having set Fire to York Minster, on the Night of the 1st of February instant, was APPREHENDED near to Hexham, on FRIDAY, the 6th inst., and lodged in the House of Correction at that place.

CHRIS. JNO. NEWSTEAD,
Clerk of the Peace for the Liberty of St. Peter, York.
Residence, York, Saturday Morning, February 7, 1829, Half past Ten o'Clock.

H. Bellerby, Printer, Gazette-Office, York.

FULL AND AUTHENTIC REPORT

OF THE

TRIAL

OF

JONATHAN MARTIN;

At the Castle of York, on Tuesday, March 31, 1829,

FOR SETTING FIRE TO YORK MINSTER;

WITH AN ACCOUNT OF THE

LIFE OF THE LUNATIC;

THE

DESTRUCTION OF THE CHOIR OF YORK CATHEDRAL

On the Second of February, 1829;

THE FLIGHT AND APPREHENSION OF THE INCENDIARY;

HIS

EXAMINATION AND COMMITMENT TO YORK CITY GAOL

THE

PROCEEDINGS AT PUBLIC MEETINGS HELD AT YORK,

In Consequence of the Fire, &c. &c.

EMBELLISHED WITH

A STRIKING LIKENESS OF MARTIN,

AND A

GROUND PLAN OF THE MINSTER.

YORK:

PUBLISHED BY H. BELLERBY, AT HIS PUBLIC LIBRARY, 13, STONGATE; AND SOLD BY ALL BOOKSELLERS.

1829.

Price One Shilling.

A Representation of the Choir of York Minster as it appeared from the Organ Screen on the 3rd of February 1829. The day after the Fire.

JONATHAN MARTIN'S COMBAT WITH THE BLACK LION
From the drawing by himself

9

It has been suggested that Jonathan Martin anticipated Sigmund Freud in that he made so much of his dreams, writing them down in his *Life of Jonathan Martin*, and interpreting them, and then taking inspiration from them in his drawings.

This is an extraordinary claim, the author thinks.

At best, Jonathan demonstrates his utter helplessness before the work of his unconscious. This must place Jonathan on the level of one of Freud's patients, rather than Freud himself. Jonathan could not anticipate Freud in any respect, and would not be revered as Freud was, and followed, and then incorporated, falsely cited, quoted when not read, abused, and repeatedly refuted.

Better the Rat Man than Freud, as the author had often thought.

Somehow, Jonathan got hold of William Hogarth's *Satan, Sin, and Death*, with sin being a woman—as usual—and naked to the waist where her body becomes foul, scaled, and serpentine. When Jonathan reproduced it at Bethlem, the woman is replaced by a bishop.

Jonathan was often found drawing bishops. A visitor in 1833 saw him drawing a bishop with seven heads—one of the many drawings that were lost.

It is not known how those heads looked and if they looked at one another and quarrelled, perhaps.

These bishops he drew were *inhumanly mangled and cruelly misinterpreted,* as Mortimer might have said of them.

They were truer bishops than those who live, as Jonathan might have replied. Or truer without as they are inside, he would have clarified.

Behold the beast as it rises up out of the sea, having seven heads and ten horns, and upon his horns ten crowns, and upon his heads the name of blasphemy. This being another line from the Book of Revelation that might have been in Jonathan's own head.

Behold the beast that was, and is not, and yet is, as Jonathan might have said to his visitor in his cell, had he had the wit to do so.

The loss of Jonathan's pictures would be a book in itself. Each picture a book. They were collectable for a while, and were strewn across the country, and passed from hand to hand, and held up as an example of madness, until their owners died, or lost interest, and Jonathan was forgotten too so that when the pictures surfaced they were no longer accompanied by an account of their origins—a visit in the 1830s, a description of the madman and how he was persuaded to part with his latest in exchange for a handshake, or a shilling. Most were genuinely mislaid between other papers that were thrown away, others were looked at and deliberately disposed of—they had become mere scribblings, odd and indecipherable and poorly executed. With no linkage to the luridly told memories of their author, they were valueless.

Hogarth's *Satan, Sin and Death* was a forerunner to the so-called horrific sublime. Or so it has been said. Its influence can be traced to John Martin's own somewhat hysterical and oddly popular creations. The effect of the horrific sublime is supposed to be one of awe and stupefaction, a kind of aesthetic pleasure before ungraspable darkness.

That the function of art and its appreciation might be to disturb and upset is one of its last justifications.

And the most abhorrent.

When Jonathan held the engraved print of *Satan, Sin and Death*, he did not experience as much awe as he had hoped. The problem was that he could always see Hogarth's brush and Hogarth at the end of it, which ruined the effect.

And his memories of Copenhagen, for instance, which were demonstrably more instructive in the effect of terror.

Jonathan's artworks might be described as disorganised. They lack overall composition, with the figure of *Death* in particular somewhat dismembered across the page. Arms and legs are frequently detached, and heads appear without bodies.

The drawings were collectable because of their derangement—a visual description of the lunatic's mind, it was thought. But the simple fact of Jonathan being in chains might account for the effects he produced. That and the large pieces of paper he was given to use. Jonathan approached the page from all angles and produced fragments of *Death* and *Satan*, and whoever else, from all directions as a result.

Jonathan was an accomplished escape artist as he had told so many for the price of one shilling, or sixpence, or eightpence. It was a reasonable precaution to fetter him at first, and then, when the fetters were taken off, the good justice and sense of doing so was proven.

Jonathan Martin, belt and gloves and wrist locked and leg locked at night attempting his escape on the 14th—this from the Bethlem hospital sub-committee minutes of 20 May 1830.

The simple fact of the use of irons must be taken into account when studying the art of early nineteenth-century lunatics, it has been written. Primitive systems of restraint were still in use and can be directly associated with their primitive aesthetics.

Jonathan himself makes the connection between his restraint and his imagery. He would write letters on the backs of his pictures. One to Lord Durham refers to a *pound of iron in each hand attached to seven more about my loins*. All that weight he suffered from morning to night and from night to morning. I have drawn this, he tells the Lord, *with my hands bound to my loins upon my seat with one knee upon the ground*.

It is still possible that Jonathan was celebrating his artistic achievement—I did even that with my hands bound to my loins, rather than excusing it—unfortunately that is all I could manage with my hands so close to my loins.

The impact of Jonathan's illness read into his drawings—his capacity to depict form deteriorates when his disorder worsens; his spatial composition becomes confused as a result of his own growing bewilderment; his brush strokes, usually firm and decisive, turn weak and uncertain as he turns weak and uncertain. Likewise, his spelling breaks down even further.

Firm and decisive lines can be found in *Jonathan Martin's Combat with the Black Lion of Hell and All His Combined Power*. This image was drawn on 26 April 1829 and again on 27 April. There are rumours of the same being drawn on 18 April, suggesting that Jonathan produced the image repeatedly and for some duration and that a whole series of drawings were assembled and lay about his cell before they were eventually dispersed, and lost.

Further evidence of his monomania, perhaps, although the author can also imagine Jonathan's pictures selling quickly, at this point, just after his trial. That meant that it made good business to go into mass production, which would be the ordinary insanity of consumption.

The giant has been described as *pea headed*, and the whole has been interpreted as no less deranged than Jonathan's other pictures, and that diagnosis is despite its more certain form. The lion's hairs are extended and curled just as Jonathan drew the sea about the ship from which he fell, was rescued, and then fell again. Except those lines do now look like hair in their proper raiment rather than a hair-grown sea. Only the locks fly too freely. This image is like a description of a lion told to someone who has never seen one. And the tongue is thick.

The giant's leg is wrapped around the back of the lion of hell so that the lion is embraced in combat and gathered in his groin.

Each day that Jonathan drew his *Combat with the Black Lion of Hell*, he held on to his tongue with the other hand and felt the scar where his tie had been cut and wondered if his tongue was a two-edged sword or its last casualty. The scar always remained tender, and when Jonathan was not feeling it with a finger, he would curl his tongue back and touch it with its tip.

One-legged lions appear frequently in his drawings, variously explained. The lion is England, Jonathan once suggested, which has one single foot remaining to stand with. *And that foot has lost a toe,* Jonathan added. *Therefore long it cannot perch.*

Or the lion is Jonathan himself—look, I only need one leg to smite England down, he said, and not even every toe of it.

Else the missing leg is accounted for by his time running out to complete the drawing—I began on the legs and only had time to finish one of them. This often happens. My jailor is superstitious, he said. Whenever I begin with my lions he comes and interrupts.

Or that he forgot the anatomy of the other three.

Or that he liked the thought of the lion hopping.

Or that he thought a lion's head looks more impressive if there is only one leg to hold it.

And, more occasionally, because he did not wish for any single image to become a key to his decipherment. *I do not wish for any single theme in my art to become my signature*, he said, or said something like that, using his typical words and his typical expressions to say it. I do not want anyone to find a signature image in my art that can be used to explain or encapsulate what I am and what I see with any kind of precision. Thus, the enigma of the lion with one foot, an inexplicable quirk, variously explained.

The author made that last one up, but there is some truth to it.

Several of the others were made up, too, and there is less truth to them.

And there is no truth at all to the suggestion that Jonathan himself did not know what he meant, and that he was confused, and this is why he came up with more than one explanation of the foot. Or, at least, if Jonathan did not know what inspired him to create, nobody else does much know what drives them much better than he did.

Which is when the author became struck by the comedy of the situation of still being in the business of wondering what Jonathan did or did not know or did or did not think.

The very first move of writing about someone who was once real is an act of betrayal, a false siege against oblivion, a means of tampering with whatever evidence remains. But it struck the author as equally indulgent to make too much of musing about the first move of writing.

On 11 April 1829, Jonathan was removed from the castle to the city gaol by order of the judge, where he spent much of his time when he was not drawing walking in the yard with his bible.

The gaol appears in the background of the battle with the black lion of hell preserved from 27 April, but not the version which survives from 26 April.

On 26 April, when Jonathan walked in the yard with his bible he looked downwards at his feet.

On 27 April, when Jonathan walked in the yard, he looked upwards at the gaolhouse exterior. Soon he would be removed to Bethlem, two hundred miles or so to the south. Looking at the gaol and drawing the gaol had become interesting, given that soon he would be gone from it.

On 28 April, he was transmitted to Bethlem.

As reported in the *Yorkshire Gazette* on 18 April, Jonathan received many visitors. *This person is amusing himself with drawing the combat of Samson and the Lion*, it is written, *and he himself is still the great lion of the city jail and is visited by numerous persons, who seem as happy if they procure his autograph as if it were that of a prince.*

A week earlier, the *York Herald* reports—*Jonathan is now very peacefully amusing himself in his prison, by drawing and painting figures which his own disordered imagination alone can portray, and madman-like, in laughing at the mischief he has effected, and exalting over the universal regret and interest thereby excited.* This on 11 April, the day of Jonathan's removal from the castle to the city gaol.

The report in the *York Herald* on 11 April and the one that follows in the *Yorkshire Gazette* on 18 April serve as free adverts, effectively, for Jonathan's drawings. *Anyone who wishes to procure a drawing should visit the gaol*, is the message in each.

Another report was written by his jailer on 13 April—*He is quiet and inoffensive in his general behaviour, subject to slight fits of excitement and depression, but requiring no personal restraint. He converses with propriety on most subjects with the exception of religion, especially with reference to the conduct of the ministers of the Established Church*—When these are introduced he quickly evinces his disordered imagination, the jailer continues, *and that he is labouring under delusion. He is perfectly well in bodily health, and has been drawing figures for his amusement for a few days past as he is in the prison alone, and for which he seems to evince very considerable natural talent.*

The jailer's report suggests that Jonathan is living in peace and seclusion, which might be cover for the truth of the situation, with the jailer making some money himself off all the visits.

Jonathan was also busy writing letters when not drawing for his visitors, or receiving these visitors, or selling his drawings to those visitors, or walking in the yard as a break from his visitors. He wrote to the Duke of Northumberland from York city gaol, having heard that the duke wanted a hermit to live seven years underground. Jonathan volunteered his own self for that, saying that he was a lone man, *I am a lone man*, he wrote, *and will exert myself to get into the situation of this underground living*. Jonathan went on to stipulate that the duke should merely furnish him with a bible, drawing materials, paper, and ink. His letter was not delivered, which meant that the duke had to look elsewhere for his hermit.

This short segment concerning the duke, his hermit, and the wishes of Jonathan Martin to spend seven years underground—rather than the rest of his life in an asylum—provided a little relief before the usual roundup of executions listed in *The Times*. These executions and various other titbits complete the column.

—John Renn is due to be executed on Monday.

—John Rutledge was hanged on Thursday.

—Edward Barnet was also hanged on Thursday.

Barnet mounted the scaffold at 11am and was *launched into eternity without any appearance of remorse, or a sense of his awful situation*—or so it was reported.

There was an inquest at Leeds, held at the Woodman Inn in view of the body of Ellen Walker, an infant aged six months. This infant came to her death by having arsenic administered by her mother out of mistake for magnesia.

Ellen Walker's mother was not hanged for that.

Jonathan would be permitted to draw regularly for two more years before his jailers at Bethlem decided it excited him too much, having given and withdrawn and given and withdrawn his drawing materials for those first, twenty-four odd months, witnessing the effect, and then, eventually, decisively, withdrawing them one last time, as they said, and then only returning his materials infrequently, each time saying as they did so that this was definitely *the last time*.

After 1830, or thereabouts, no further drawings appear to have been preserved or much produced, and the doing of them is replaced by Jonathan's repeated complaint at not being able.

Two days before he died in 1838, Jonathan asked for and was given permission to draw again. It became Bethlem lore that the drawing killed him, which caused some inmates to commence drawing and others to cease drawing, depending upon their intentions.

This is what Richard, his son, records—*He had got permission to draw a little, which he had not been allowed to do for a long time. I left him paper, etc., and he began with eagerness, and must have worked very hard at it; for he would not get the paper until Tuesday morning, and on Wednesday it was that he felt himself ill, and gave his drawing and everything up to the keeper, and said he was assured he would not require them anymore, and he would only read his Bible. In a short time he had half covered a large sheet of drawing paper with a serpent, lions, archers shooting, and other things which I do not remember as I have not the drawing yet.*

The inmates did not know about the trick of drawing a serpent, lions, archers shooting, and the other things Richard could not remember, or there would have been a decisive study of these things in the artwork of Bethlem inmates in that year and those that followed. Instead, those who took up drawing, produced what they thought Jonathan would have drawn, these productions being many and various depending on how each lunatic understood the mind of their fellow and newly deceased companion.

A study of these drawings would produce a rich insight into the multiple versions of Jonathan already existing at that time, the author feels.

The hospital staff complained that Jonathan only drew York Minster. *Whenever this indulgence was extended to him, he invariably occupied his time in drawing sketches of the cathedral,* the governors reported, *which threw him into a state of very considerable excitement.* Only one drawing of the Minster survives, suggesting that almost every sketch was destroyed, or the governors had a peculiar way of seeing, overlooking the serpents and the bishops and the other figures, able to glimpse only architectural features—walls, archways, towers—which were all presumed elements of the building he torched. The governors were very proud of their own building, too—its walls, archways, towers, and so on.

The governors feared that Jonathan made a habit of listening to and interpreting the dreams of his inmates, and that most dreams he interpreted as dreams against the establishment.

He causes the lunatic to focus on the formlessness of his nocturnal peregrinations, one notes in his diary.

We have found the lunatics of late telling each other of their dreams and nodding with mutual enthusiasms, writes another.

The visitor who spotted Jonathan drawing a bishop with seven heads in 1833, also mentions *bituminous breath* and *an enormous crocodile*. The bishop is running into its jaws, and this despite the bishop's many heads.

It is not clear from the grammar of the sentence whose breath this was, if it was the breath of the bishop heads, or the breath of the crocodile, which smelled so awfully. This seemed a minor point, but the author became caught up with it. The sentence reads, *drawing a bishop with seven heads, under the influence of absolute fatalism, undaunted by its bituminous breath, rushing into the open jaws of a colossal crocodile.*

The author wonders if most writing could be of this sort, a kind of perseveration over points of interest vested unduly with importance to avoid all the more pressing problems that cannot be written down, or are only written down on the condition that they become diversions themselves.

From the perspective of the writer, anyone other than a writer who wishes to convey their so-called *rich interior* is suffering from inexplicable urges.

Of Jonathan Martin it has been written—*It is not easy to understand why this almost illiterate man, long before the deed that ensured his fame, felt so strong a need to communicate his private conception of the world.*

The author would name the source but feels queasy about pointing to any particular person for holding such views, when these views are so widespread.

There is an association presumed between being illiterate and being intellectually mute; either the illiterate is intellectually mute or that the illiterate ought to be, and effectively is.

This is the conceit. It is rarely stated so baldly.

The desire to communicate ideas beyond the reach of an individual's voice, to speak further than a shout is heard, is surely only cultivated by those intellectually driven and intellectually sanctioned devices which enable it—such as books.

Which means any technology that enables communication beyond these intellectually sanctioned means is suspicious and tends to illiteracy.

The advantage of books is that they are so tedious and long to write, which takes a special type of training, or self-belief, a sense of entitlement over the written word.

Entitlement over the written word—the author wondered how that definition might fare against all other definitions of what it means to be literate.

The author suspects that this line of enquiry is another of those diversions.

The author is beginning to wonder what exactly the author is hoping to achieve.

The author is thankful that Jonathan Martin has left so many remnants of his life to become preoccupied with.

Jonathan Martin's skill at drawing is described in the *Yorkshire Gazette* around the time of the trial as *exhibiting extraordinary marks of uninstructed talent, mixed with frenzy and wildness.*

The visitor to his cell in 1833 is less impressed—*The artist disappointed me: he was crude, ignorant, impotent. His sketch was a mere exaggerated matter of fact, madly conceived, and contemptibly executed.* This was the visitor who spotted the picture of the bishop with the seven heads, and the crocodile, and the bituminous breath. It is hard to understand how that could be described as an *exaggerated matter of fact*, given the visitor's contempt for the inmate and what the inmate saw in the world about him.

The Duke of Orleans rated his art highly enough to buy it, or someone did, that someone having been introduced to Jonathan Martin as the Duke. This was not unusual—the visit, not the accolade—he was visited by numerous members of the aristocracy. Jonathan, together with a few other enticing Bedlamites, was on their circuit.

The Duke was purchasing a picture of Jonathan's for his cousin the King of France, so Jonathan believed. It is not clear what the picture depicted, or why the King wanted it, or at least why the Duke thought that the King might want it. This was 1829.

The Duke of Orleans reigned after the King's son who reigned after his father. The King's son holds the record of the shortest in history—about twenty minutes—after which he, too, abdicated. This was 1830. The honour is shared with the Crown Prince of Portugal who also reigned for twenty minutes, seventy-eight years later. The Crown Prince was mortally wounded, which seems a better excuse.

Other similarly short reigns have also been had, but with the difference that nobody present was holding a watch to it or had a watch to hold.

Or bothered to record the short-lived incumbent. There was a scuffle, they might have said, and left it at that.

The Duke may have noticed numerous prints about Jonathan's cell and, if he had an eye for it, would have seen some likeness between those prints and Jonathan's own creations. All were suitably adapted, of course, to Jonathan's habits of seeing.

Jonathan made a point of adapting images from other sources to his own ends. There is nothing left to do but adapt and distort what already exists when the work of creation—the world in its entirety—is over, and any remaining effort in that direction is presumptuous to excess.

The author feels that Jonathan was onto something here. It might also be added that the world, as it exists, is also busy enough adapting and distorting itself.

When John Martin visited his brother at Bethlem, he smiled benevolently at his works and then sent envoys to gather up any prints of his own work that he had seen that might be abused as Jonathan abused images, by making them his own.

In 1825, a full five years before Jonathan did his drawing, John was publishing his own *Satan, Sin and Death*. It was more lucrative than Jonathan's, since John had his work serialised and was paid 2000 guineas up front. This was a huge amount in the old money and Jonathan probably heard all about how much money John made and how much his *Satan, Sin and Death* was admired. And yet, it is clearly Hogarth's painting, and not John's print, that Jonathan was working from. If Jonathan had his brother's print in his cell, he turned it over or put it aside, leaving John's envoys to collect the print, notice the subject of Jonathan's latest drawing, and report this frustrating fact to the brother.

The author is struck again by the malice of calling one son Jonathan and the other John.

It might not be malice, but the author's own irritation at the closeness of the names, which makes for confusion when the author is feeling tired.

Several references may be found later that century to the *lunatic* John Martin, or *Mad Martin*. With Jonathan forgotten, the rumour of madness was attached to his brother. Even if one had been the son of a perverse and evil woman and the other the son of a woman related to the holiest mother on earth, it would still be easy to confuse them.

Extreme holiness can look like extreme evil, the author writes, taking some godly pleasure in that.

The evidence against John being mad—John, the Artist, could not be described as mad, it has been said, as he raised a large family, was financially successful, and functioned well in society.

John is also portrayed as elegant, educated, and accomplished. Further evidence, it would seem, against his being mad.

John Martin's fame might be characterised as extraordinary, or grotesque, depending upon who is doing the describing.

And temporary, depending again on which century is doing the looking.

John Martin had the unusual privilege among artists of being enormously popular when he lived and then less so, once he died.

He produced spectacular artworks to gawp at and has been compared, in his fame, and in the impact of his work, to the effect generated by Hollywood extravaganzas. This caused the author to wonder why anyone would write after John Martin or after cinema, and then remember that the purpose of writing—archaic as it may be—is to investigate what writing can still do that the canvas, or the screen, cannot do.

The effect of John's paintings is to remind the civilized that all civilizations crumble, in time, and so to hold onto theirs with greater tenacity and self-regarding assurance. This is what he dubbed *the perspective of feeling*.

When John wrote, *the picture shall make more noise than any picture ever did before,* he did not know that Jonathan would later say, *I have made as much noise as Bonaparte ever did.*

And my brother, he might have added.

During the blaze at York, it is said that a lady, who was seeing it and *while admiring the sublime and terrific spectacle,* then remarked— *What a subject for John Martin.* She did not yet know it was his brother who had done it. This must have irked John some, or would have done if John had been stood there beside her.

She was quoted in the *Yorkshire Gazette* two pages after Jonathan was quoted in his boast. This was still 1829.

One of the prints retrieved by John's envoy was *Joshua Commanding the Sun to Stand Still.* This was for the better killing of the Amorites.

Another was *The Fall of Nineveh.* Jonathan wrote to his brother suggesting he might do better to paint the fall of London, about which he had dreamt, and if he would not paint it, perhaps he should go see it.

John dedicated the 1830 print of *The Fall of Nineveh* to the King of France, Charles X. This was the same month as the July Revolution, and the abdication of Charles—after much weeping—and the twenty-minute reign of his son. The irony was not missed on Jonathan, who would tell anyone with ears about his brother's uncanny and unwitting prophecy. My brother, he said, might be a celebrated artist, but he cannot tell artistry from prophecy or cannot see, as I can see, the prophecy of his artistry. My brother, Jonathan said, likes to draw pictures of doom only so that he can live more comfortably as the guineas pile up around him.

Some might consider this ungrateful, given how John paid for his trial from that pile of guineas. Jonathan saw it as justified, given that John had also, in the same gesture, forked out to certify his dear younger brother, a Bedlamite.

Artistic prophecy is nothing, Jonathan went on, alongside artistic effect, which is what some have called a self-fulfilling prophecy—identified after the fact—but I would prefer to call my self-fulfilling fate. My picture carried to the King by the Duke is an example of that, he said, and might be related directly to the abdication and, more specifically to the weeping.

These are not Jonathan words, naturally.

10

If there are any drawings *or other little articles*, John wrote, the keeper may have them and my nephew will hand them over.

The nephew, Richard, wrote his own letter to the Governors of Bethlem, requesting his father's last drawings. It is not clear which way things were handed, or what was their fate.

Richard would be dead soon after.

John made it to 1854.

As did Ann.

The other Richard was already dead.

The eldest brother, William the Philosopher, died in 1851.

His last days were passed in comfort at his brother John's house at Chelsea— so it is written in the *Dictionary of National Biography*.

Despite his quackery and buffoonery, William Martin possessed much ingenuity as a mechanician, it also reports.

In 1814, he married *a celebrated dressmaker*, as he called her, whom he also describes as *an inoffensive woman*. She died in 1832 and left him with some capital to live by, initially fairly well, and eventually not so well, which means from one can of salted beans to the next.

Salted beans contain *all the elements of nutriment required by human beings*, wrote William. This is not recorded in the *Dictionary of National Biography*.

In that same year he founded the so-called *Martinean Society, based, in opposition to the Royal Society, upon the negation of the Newtonian system of gravitation*.

He signed his lucubrations, *Wm. Martin, Nat. Phil. And Poet*.

The author notes that William also signed off, *WM. Martin, Anti-Newtonian*, depending upon the circumstance.

Towards the end of his life, William *affected extreme singularity of attire*, the dictionary records, *and hawked his books and exhibited his inventions among the Northumbrian miners*.

The entry for William the Philosopher ends with a long list of his various publications, most of them pamphlets, all self-published.

The last of these was entitled, *The Philosopher's Just Charge against Bishops, Priests and Deacons*. It prophesied the end of the world in the twenty-first century.

His hat was made of tortoise shell and was mounted with brass. This was his last hat, the one he wandered about Newcastle with in his last remaining years. The rest of the man was inside a military surtout—a kind of greatcoat—buttoned up to the throat.

Gratified to meet you, sir, is what he said if anyone spoke to him. To which he added, *I am the Philosophical Conqueror of All Nations, that is what I am, and this is my badge*. At this point William unbuttoned his coat to reveal a medal as large as a saucer, hung about his neck.

And then produced one of his latest pamphlets about how the Philosopher had solved all manner of problems, most of them eminently practical.

William was a practical man. He even sustained injuries in a practical way.

In 1840, William stepped from a railway carriage when the train was still moving. There were other injuries too as well as the two ribs he broke that day. The old man was a mess, said the porter who first gathered him up. Look at you, what a mess you are, were the words that William first heard after the cracking of his ribs. I will write to the Railway Directors about this, William said by reply. You watch me, I will do it, he told the porter. And promptly did so, with his free arm, demanding they impose a fine of six shillings and two pence—costly for some passengers, affordable to others—for anyone who left the carriage as he had done, and did not wait for it to stop. William, it is said, was on the side of the poor and saw to it that his proposed deterrent, a fine, was precisely calculated and would keep the poor safe by preferment. Such was his cleverness.

When, in 1841, the Queen appointed a William Martin to be Lord Chief Justice of Australia, this other William, the one with the tortoiseshell hat, was approached and told of it. To which William, brother of Jonathan, replied that he was *not altogether satisfied* with his appointment—I am an old man in the afternoon of life, but if this is the case, I will not wish to offend her.

This queen gave birth to several haemophiliacs, a point of note, apparently, but still nothing in the shedding of blood she oversaw.

William did some violence too by royal command, and later in life by his own. In 1846, he was attacked by a ruffian—which means, by someone unknown, presumed to be poor—and, keeping a keen eye, as he put it, William cut him smart and hard.

William joined the Northumberland Militia in 1795, assembled some years previous to curb rioting and such like, or fire on looters and arsonists, or be praised for holding fire on looters and arsonists, whichever it happened to be.

Just before he joined the Militia, William went to Hexham to visit his parents. John was still a child in frocks, and Richard, the other brother, was serving his time as a currier and stank some because of it. There is no mention of Jonathan. Perhaps he was in the woods or already at the Roman Wall where an extraordinary number of Roman penises may be found, carved.

Renowned for his swordsmanship, William was engaged to teach some of the officers how to parry, and lunge, and so forth— the author has entirely made this up, knowing nothing of the sport. This teaching offended the battalion fencing instructor, who challenged William to meet him on Sunderland moor, saying that he had never found any better than himself, for which boast the fencing instructor was cut twelve times. I cut him twelve times, William recalls, without receiving a cut myself. This was all watched by a crowd of the grenadiers and a celebrated pugilist.

There was also a challenge by a well-revered fencer from some Irish dragoons, who happened to be at the same billet. This was in 1796, somewhere between Lincoln and Norwich. The man was another self-proclaimed master at the science of cutting up opponents, but William disabled him at the sword arm without receiving a cut himself.

At Norwich they had a riot with the Warwickshire Militia, not having organised a riot by proxy, with either William or the pugilist serving as the Northumberland arm of violence. The Northumberland Militia was removed to Colchester as its penance, where, by order of the King, there was to be no assembling of people in companies to exceed two or three, and no one was to speak against the King or the soldiers in their twos and threes, or otherwise they would be informed against, again by order of His Majesty. But soon enough there was fun to be had here too. All kinds of men were assembled, William writes, both horse and foot, and artillery also, to the amount of several thousands, that is to say, too many for twos and threes, unless these thousands were to be distributed across the county. There was a fencing match at that place, and five fencing masters and master instructors were preparing for contest, with all the officers lined up in front of the rest. Where have we Martin, our celebrated fencer, Captain Leaves said to the rest of the officers, and they made enquiry to left and right among the men, with some saying he was last seen with a net and a rod, and had gone to fish, and that he had feared being in a company of two, lest it become a three and that three become a four. And so, five parties were sent to the five known rivulets in the vicinity. William was found fishing as predicted and was retrieved from holding that rod so he could lance about with another, settling one instructor after the next—these conquests being in twos—without receiving a single cut from any of them. For this he was rewarded by being carried aloft and announced with three huzzas at the end of every street of Colchester. That was Colchester's own penance for profiting so well from all the drinking and the eating these troops had been doing, that and all the piss in the alleys, and the side fights, and so on.

That William fell from the train as an old man was hard in a way because, in his youth, he was a champion not simply at fencing, but also at leaping. This forgotten sport involves one man challenging another to see who does the biggest.

William was drawing in his tent one day, so the story goes, when his friend, the famous pugilist, asked him to come to the booth with him and have a goodly amount of ale. Come drink with us, said William Buteland—another William, the author notes, which confuses things, and so the author decided to opt for pugilist instead. Well, this pugilist comes in and says, with the tent flapping all about, have some ale, William, to which William the future Philosophical Conqueror of Nations replies, I'm not thirsty, which is a strange thing to say to a pugilist and a fellow comrade and member of His Majesty's Killing Arm, so William relented and went for the ale, and along the way was told of the challenge set down by a grenadier from the Nottingham Militia who said not a man in William's own Militia could leap against him and win, and that, given William's renown as a good leaper, he should do the leaping for the brigade and prove the Nottingham man wrong. Which he did. The stakes were agreed at a guinea a side, and William asked what kind of leap, and was answered by his challenger, *a running leap*, which is a kind of leap that William considered not a fair leap, and demanded a standing leap. The ground was selected, a cut was made, and each man did his leaping. William's leap was measured four yards and four inches, which was thirteen more than his rival. In leaping terms, that is a good margin.

After that, there was a storm which blew down their tents and broke their poles, and they marched with those tents, poles missing, to Hull, where more poles were found, and William invented his flying machine.

Then more tramping up and down the north and east of England, and some time spent in Cambridge where William, so he reports, *never saw a place so well-stocked with lewd women*. Somehow, his eyes missed the lewd men too, or he was one of them and did not think of them, or himself, as lewd, but really just men or a man about his business. In any case, I soon came to know, writes William, that the collegians were very clever at hauling them into their upper chambers by ropes.

Then they marched to Alnwick, where there was a challenge from the local leaping champion, who was defeated. The day after that William was discharged after seven years' service, several sword fights, and all the leaping, of course.

Which was when he went to Haydon Bridge to visit his parents and invent a paddle boat to solve all river boating dilemmas, or some of them, which was not a small amount given how much bile is spilt in the waterways around England, getting up and then down, and around bends, and so on, these rivers tending to be meandering, and irksome, and ponderous, and slow.

Then, and thereafter, William wrought at the ropery as a ropemaker, and began to study perpetual motion, and discovered it after thirty-seven different inventions. This discovery has, William writes, *proved all philosophers imposters, and false men, and deceivers of mankind.*

Or, as he elsewhere describes them, *deceivers of the people*, who, by their conjectures and their teachings and their writings, *made a complete nursery for foolish infidels and servants of the devil.*

Or, again, a little differently, *complete professors of lies and nonsense.*

The clue for perpetual motion was already in Genesis for anyone who cared to look.

And the Lord God formed man of the dust of the ground, and breathed into his nostrils the breath of life, and man became a living soul.

Ergo, *breath* is the secret of perpetual motion.

Or as William might say—*Breath* is the great Perpetual Cause. *Breath* is the *Primum Mobile*—and so on, this William inhaling every so often with the proclamations.

That the great clue recorded in Genesis has been overlooked for so many centuries, millennia indeed, owes not simply to the inadequacy of all philosophers—which means, the failure of every philosopher since before philosophy was named as such. This owes to the imperfection of all readers and all societies, which means many readers and many societies—raised and died—would need to pass until William, the Englishman, sat down and read those words.

It is widely believed, writes William, that England will have to be the highly-honoured school for the whole terrestrial globe. Well now it is true, he thought.

This passage in Genesis has hitherto been slightly noticed, William writes. Or rather, indeed, it has been entirely overlooked by our great Philosophers, from whom the Great Almighty has thought proper to conceal this important Discovery until mankind had arrived at a more perfect state—the author enjoys these odd capitalisations and retains them. It is made a matter of even greater admiration, William continues, to illuminate, by His Divine Assistance, the mind of a poor, simple individual, *favoured by education only in a small degree*, with light sufficient to make this great Discovery.

These were William's words, the author notes, so as not to forget the difference.

As are these words—*an important lesson this to mankind*, not to depend altogether on their learning, for learning will not confer genius. If otherwise, our Blessed Lord and Saviour Jesus Christ would not have chosen poor, illiterate fishermen to preach his Holy Word.

Actually, William goes on, *He only intended thereby*—this *thereby* referring to the use of illiterates—*to magnify His Holy Name, to display His Wonderful Power, and to render the Works of God the more astonishing*. Which might be read, the author thinks, as a rationale for the exploitation of illiterates and not their ascension.

Demonstrably, then, William's discovery of perpetual motion is one such astonishing work, given to the world by a man who would be otherwise overlooked for not having the right qualities nor training, or the right diction, or the proper taste in hats, for having spent his childhood chasing birds from sheep.

Having discovered the passage in Genesis and having understood it rightly for the first time, William's challenge was merely to harness this breath—probably not the right metaphor, the author thinks, it being overly Newtonian.

William's challenge, the author begins again, was to find out how to have that breath blow at him, to open his nostrils and receive it, and his mechanism too. I wished to have that breath blow at me, and be downwind of it, and place my devices in its path, said William, and conjure little nostrils for those devices.

This breath William renames AIR so as to convince lay and religious alike.

This AIR, writes William, is the real Cause of the Perpetual Motion, without which neither man nor beast can live, vegetation nor the fishes of the sea exist. The tides ebb and flow because of it, and so do the planets perform their functions.

The Moon only causes the Spring Tide, explains William, and the AIR does the rest of them. If the moon was indeed the cause of these *daily* phenomena, as Sir Isaac Newton states, he ought to have proved her the cause of *all things*, which he did not do because he could not. The Moon must submit to the AIR like everything else, it is not her privilege to avoid it.

William assembles his *General Observations on Air* so that the basics of it covers not more than a single page—

What is the occasion of Music? ... AIR

—of Man's Life? ... AIR

—of Trees and Vegetation? ... AIR

—of Animal Existence? ... AIR

—of Perpetual Motion? ... AIR

—of the Ebbing and Flowing of the Tides? ... AIR

—of Attraction? ... AIR

—of Repulsion? ... AIR

—of Electricity? ... AIR

—of Fire and Water? ... AIR

—of Thunder and Lightning? ... AIR

—of Wood and Stone? ... AIR

—of the Planets and their Motions? ... AIR

—is the great Preserver? ... AIR

—is the great Destroyer? ... AIR

On 4 January 1807, William set his machine going in Newcastle—the Duke of Northumberland was most entranced—and again on 4 January 1808 in the Metropolis, where it was exhibited at No. 28 on the Haymarket. Here it was visited for years by the finest nobility and gentry of the kingdom, who could not fathom it, and searched in side rooms, and casements, and below the floorboards if they could be listened at, for the secret engine that must surely be the origin of his illusion. None could find it, of course, because it was run by the Perpetual Motion, by the primary agent, the great cause of all things, AIR, which divine providence had seen fit to reveal at last. The great Sun itself shines because of it, and without it all organised bodies cease to exist. The Earth rotates and floats upon it too, as may be exemplified by gently blowing a pea on the end of a tobacco pipe shank held vertical. The Earth is the pea, and the pea is the Earth, each oscillates, and if the pea is wet, it will oscillate with minor tides upon its surface. It has no need of another pea, which would be its moon.

The temerity of William's pamphlet-writing strikes the author as extraordinary, of course, but not alien, since every book which claims to have discovered something and wishes to offer that discovery to the world has something of William's pride.

The author pauses for a moment to list some statements—

Every philosopher hitherto sought answers and from each answer derived a question. That was the way of it.

It was their way of putting the cart before the horse—a crude and commonplace saying for a crude and commonplace practice— which means putting the answer before the question.

Even those stating they were more interested in questions than answers began with answers too—this being their answer.

Every question was thereby contrived by way of the answers that were already presumed. And so those questions, and those answers, were false and mistaken.

But this period in which the answer had dominance has now ended.

With the true and fundamental question now appearing, and it being AIR, all answers may be organised by way of it.

The author thinks this is what William intended, that this was the logic of his argument.

Everything known and accepted must be unknown and become unacceptable—this seems to be William's argument too.

Newton was 898,651 times wide of the truth, in relation to the Sun, for instance.

Or 899,326 times wide, depending on which of William's works is consulted.

In any case, Newton's error stands, and that is no way to enlighten the aged or the young.

With the discovery of AIR, man will no longer need to be sceptical about his place in the universe or about the grounds of its motion, nor can man doubt any longer the principles that must underly his orderly living. Or if he remains sceptical, he will be unreasonably sceptical. Only unreasonable sceptics can exist, following William. The reasonable sceptic ceases to exist when the fundament of AIR is arrived at.

The Sun will be seen as an object in motion because it must be due to the Perpetual Motion. With this new perception, the Sun can still remain at the centre of things, but that centre is a moveable one, and God shall be found in his seat at its radiant middle, moving with it.

And the Sun is no more a tremendous burning globe of fire than any other planet is burning, or it would diminish, and burn out its fuel, and cause the Planetary System to cease, and all to end. The Sun has its own winters, too, and there are wintering places on the surface of the Sun, just as there are summer places. All warmth and all light is merely the irradiation of the Great God, its heavenly resident, the Great Creator of the Universe.

Hell is simply where His radiance diminishes and may be found at the furthest reaches from the Sun and in the shadows of large objects. The Regions of Darkness are boundless and illimitable, and were a cannonball to be sent flying in that direction, and should it travel for a million years and with undiminished velocity, that ball would still be in transit. The Heavens have a boundary about them—this is what Heavenly means—whereas Hell has none. Hell has neither depth nor height, end nor sides. No circumference bounds those doleful shades. This is why the

Holy Scriptures term it the Bottomless Pit, from which emerge all combination of creatures and horrors imaginable and yet to be imagined. And as it is with the Heavens and Hell, so too with human existence on earth, and the necessities of order and enclosure and law, and the regions of menace beyond them.

Attempts to produce a machine that runs by Perpetual Motion have been legion, and recur across centuries, and strike the author as a recurring dream, a manifestation of ordered systems themselves that, in their enclosed spaces, would have it believed there is sufficient vivacity to endure, that walling life in will sustain it better than not, that they will propel themselves onward, and defy the dissipation of energies, the death instinct built into their complex machines, which comes crawling, eventually, from within every closed community, to rot from its innards out.

What are Blazing Comets, writes William, but not Planets like our own, thrown by the Most High from the Seat of His Glory, whom, by the power of His word, can doom to destruction any part of the Universe he pleases. Yet even these victims will travel around the celestial seat, which is the Sun, and do so endlessly in their eccentric orbits, thus showing that all things obey a higher order—His design—and that Godly Wrath is orderly too, and that all is orderly, even as it burns and trails the waste of that burning across the sky because every object returns on its own self perpetually in the encompassing hold of his Reason.

The stars cannot be Suns, for if there were a plurality of Suns, there would be as many Gods, that is to say, there would be Gods without number. And in their countless radiances, these Gods would leave no place for Hell, writes William.

This has to be one of the more curious arguments for the one and true God, the author feels.

That Joshua had the Sun be still so the Amorites might be slaughtered is no refutation of my discovery, claimed William.

Although the Sun did stand still and all the other planets also, they nonetheless still oscillated like the pea on the pipe, and so their Perpetual Motion was preserved, kept ready for that moment when the Almighty Fiat would send the Sun, His heavenly habitation, to resume its course.

The immense accumulation of ice around the North Pole, writes William, changing the subject, occurred some centuries back and has occasioned a very great irregularity of the seasons. Around 1815, Providence, for the good of the poor and for the purpose of making the seasons more regular and, consequently, the fruits of the Earth more plentiful, was pleased to detach prodigious quantities of it. This allows AIR, the great cause of things, more free circulation around the Pole and will tend, in no small degree, to afford us more regular seasons for a considerable time to come.

His Majesty's Killing Fleet must boil its timbers in seawater as a provision against dry rot—this being one of William's other gifts to humanity.

And the invention of a life-jacket, which uses AIR to keep afloat, anointed with bees-wax and tallow, which will render it perfectly tight—Having lost the drawing of this contrivance out of my pocket in London streets, says William, on my return thither in 1807, and passing the Tower, I saw one Daniel, of Wapping, exhibiting my Life Preserver to the multitude. He was bobbing about in the Thames to the admiration of the crowd. With a loud voice, I claimed it as mine, but without effect.

And the invention of a safety lamp for the coal mines, that was William too. This one, the Martin lamp, would not, in fact, ignite the fatal hydrogen gas as other so-called safety lamps were doing—or so it might be presumed, with none surviving each conflagration to tell. Sir Humphry Davy's was by far the best of these lamps, and so the worst of them, being adopted as the best of them more frequently than the worst, and so causing, by that measure, more deaths of a type less endurable than the ordinary deaths that the miners were used to.

With Davy's lamp, the miners were even more unsuspecting than before, that before being when the miners used lesser lamps, lamps that were not yet safety lamps, and which made no attempt by their design to protect the flame and keep the flame inside where it belonged. The miners feared more for their lives with the lesser lamps than with Davy's, fearful as they used those murder lamps, as they called them, that at any moment the invisible gas released by the coal, in the pit, would ignite and burn them all up with it. This way of dying was a better death than a death by Davy's lamp since Davy had convinced them that with a Davy's lamp, death would not happen, and so it would be an undeserved death when it did.

All of which meant, or was taken to mean, that not even precautions could save the miners, and their world could not be improved—this belief, the author thinks, this conviction that the best the world can be has already been arrived at, recurs throughout history, or recent history, and must be treated as another strain of millenarianism.

Davy later improved his lamp, of course, and did so by thieving particulars from the Martin design, and the conviction returned for a short while that the lives of the suffering and downtrodden can indeed be improved, and technology is at the seat of it— another strain of millenarianism, the author feels, which promises betterment and defers annihilation and the fear of annihilation to a future date.

William also invented a contrivance to better convey coal from the pit mouth to the screen—just raise the pit mouth and lay a cast metal rail-road from it for a rolly to run upon, William said. It is unthinkable that the miners had not yet thought of it, said his brother John, and Richard agreed, both being there with William at that time to admire him say so. This plan was stolen too.

In the year 1814, returning to claim another invention as his, one from 1806—a pit shaft fan—William found them taking the full corf of coal to the screen upon my plan. Thus was I robbed of the merit of two valuable discoveries in one single pit.

The invention from 1806 fell upon the news of thirty-two men having lost their lives in the pit, that and the general exhaustion William then felt at cracking his brain upon the Perpetual Motion problem. The method he contrived was on the principle of a winnowing machine, made larger, to fan AIR down the pit in great quantities. The man of the pit to whom William spoke of his plan said there was something prophetic to how William said the word AIR, which got William thinking, and he walked from the pit, forgetting the ventilator plan, pronouncing AIR, and then AIR again, with different intonations—the secret of Perpetual Motion was discovered the year after.

When William returned in 1814 to claim his fan and his reward, he told the miners that the plan originated with him, and that they should pay him, and that even if they built a long tube and placed a fan on top of it, and that tube was as high as St. Paul's, still the invention would be his.

William reports a long dream—something about running naked from a majestic lion in some woods and getting licked all over—which he then interprets point by point so that everything which occurred is allegorical and predictive, where the licking specifically portends, as William writes, that the Government will, at some point of my life, take notice of me and my inventions.

After confounding the visitors to No. 28 on the Haymarket for a couple of decades and having sold the machine there in any case, William eventually revealed the secret of his mechanism—a long tube.

This tube must be let communicate with the external air, outside of the building, led inward to a receiver which will confine that air. This tube runs below the floor so as to conceal it. Into the top part of the receiver enters another tube, the width of a man's finger—which finger, and which man is not specified—which is the nostril. This is connected to a pendulum, the pendulum to a chain, and the chain to the spring of a watch. A rivet. An ivory ball. A hook. All of it ingeniously constructed. And the motion will begin of its own accord and never cease.

In another dream, the lion is under the matrimonial bed and emerges for a bit of meat, which William gives him, after which it returns to the underside commotions, which rock the whole, causing William and his wife to fall all over and about. This dream is again interpreted at length, none of which involves any further mention of his wife.

11

Everything I have written was necessary to write, writes William.

At Wallsend, we heard of islands growing in the sea like a parcel of mushrooms, and I refuted it, telling and then writing against those sailors who came home and told all who did not know better. This falsehood was done away with at its birth, unlike the many others that have become rooted and take more tearing at and tenacity.

I did actually dream of writing only from the bible, assembling each book I wrote from quotes and adding nothing more, said William.

Cursed is he that addeth or diminisheth my Word, would be the first of them.

And so it would go on from there.

I imagined all writing would be like this since no other book can be written, or should be written, when all has been said that should be said, and anything more is a debasement of it. And a presumption too that there are other creators worthy of creating alongside or at least after the almighty Creator, and that they can make things new themselves, as men and not as Gods, or as men as if they were Gods.

But when I saw how many men, for so many centuries, have presumed to do both, adding and diminishing from His Word, adding and diminishing for years upon years and centuries after that, I saw it fit to diminish those who added, and add against what they had done, to compensate for all the diminishment.

Which is why it is justifiable that I write, wrote William, because this writing of mine is not creation, but correction.

About politics, William has little to say because evils here are much simpler to refute. *A tory cannot be a spiritual-minded man. Nor can he be a man of sound judgement. They are all servants of Beelzebub, the devil,* he writes.

The author knows clarifying words are needed to explain that the word *tory* has changed in terms of its referent but is overcome with laziness and has left those words off the page.

No restraints upon writing can be found with those who seek to profit by it. The profit motive among authors, and certainly among publishers, is the secret of their Perpetual Motion, or one secret of it, and the reason for so much noise and not enough silence. The clamour for readers is another reason, or *Primum Mobile*, as William might put it, for so much repetitive scribbling and the afterlife of exhausted forms, such as the novel. But it is still too easy to blame one and then the other for the systematic production of safe, unnecessary fictions, the author feels, and wonders if the worst of all causes is the desire, felt not only by authors, yet worst exemplified by them, to have the universe answer and confirm their existence.

To switch texts, the writer of *A Full and Authentic Report of the Trial of Jonathan Martin* is not revealed, which simplifies its motive, and frees up the present author's mind for reading it. Sold at one shilling and printed in the year of the trial for maximum sales, it includes *An Account of the Life of the Lunatic* and another of his flight and apprehension and capture.

This book has another one of those very long titles, characteristic of the time.

Jonathan's life would have sunk into its grave almost unknown and unregarded, the *Full and Authentic Report* begins, if not for the fire at York. Just like Eratosthenes, it adds.

There seems to be some confusion here, in the opening sentence of the *Full and Authentic Report*, between Eratosthenes the Beta—known as such for always coming second in his endeavours—and Herostratus the Incendiary, who confessed on the rack that the only reason he torched the Temple of Artemis was to have his name recorded in history. Eratosthenes torched nothing, or if he torched something, nobody found out.

A law was enacted to condemn the memory of Herostratus and make it forbidden to mention the name of Herostratus in person, or in writing.

There could be no better enticement.

The survival of the name testifies to the limits of the law. Historical erasure is typically more chaotic, and so the only law to enact it would be one that was less direct and does not forbid this or that but prompts chaos, and upon that chaos, the involution of memory.

The Temple of Artemis was another of the Seven Wonders of the World, alongside the Colossus of Rhodes already mentioned.

The *Full and Authentic Report* itemises what was destroyed with a handy ground plan included so that readers might better ascertain and appreciate the extent of injury.

The roof of the centre aisle, of exquisite workmanship—entirely destroyed.

The interior from the organ screen to the altar screen, also, completely consumed.

Including the beautiful canopies which adorned the prayer house, the stalls, galleries, cathedra, pulpit, altar rails, etcetera.

The plate glass in the altar screen—nearly all broken.

And the following monuments, damaged either from the falling roof, or by the heat of the flames—

—The Earl of Strafford's elegant white marble monument, reparable.

—Those to Archbishops Dolbeine, Hutton, and Sharp, damaged but reparable too.

Dolbeine has lost a finger as has one of his cherubs lost a wing. The reclining bishop—always portly, sumptuous in his attire—remained placid in his outlook.

Hutton was generally charred but otherwise unaffected in his own semi-recumbent state. Unlike the flowing extravagance of Dolbeine, Hutton endured it with characteristic stiffness.

Sharp retained his alert posture despite the debris which covered his head.

—The sarcophagus of the Finch family, considerably shattered.

—Archbishop Matthew, deprived of his fingers and toes and otherwise mutilated.

—A table tomb to the memory of Frances Cecil, Countess of Cumberland, laid prostate and totally destroyed.

—Archbishop Scrope's gothic monument, considerably damaged and marble cracked.

Scrope was beheaded in 1405. He asked that it be done with five strokes of the axe, in memory of the Five Wounds of Christ.

The author finds this hard to believe.

Before he was beheaded, Scrope was paraded through York, riding backwards on a mule.

The author can well believe that.

—Archbishop Frewin's monument, which stands twenty feet high, partially injured.

—Archbishop Rotherham's solid table tomb, totally destroyed, and the table part, six inches thick, much broken.

—Archbishop Sterne's monument, considerably injured.

Sterne was protected by his canopy, rather like a drawn back stage-curtain for the big reveal. His two cherubs outside fared less well. Sterne kept his bored expression—some would view it as the vacancy of holiness—whereas the cherubs look, and still seem, considerably alarmed.

—Archbishop Bowett's sepulchral shrine repaired only a few years back, a complete ruin.

—Archbishop Sewall's monument, totally destroyed.

In the north side aisle partial destructions to Rev. Richard Thompson's, Sir George Savile's, and Dr. Swinburne's marble. Very serious damage to Admiral Medley's monument, and in the case of two monuments by the gate, total destruction.

The clustered columns of the choir in the side aisles were also considerably defaced, and the capitals too.

All the curiosities kept in the vestries survived, including the large Horn of Ulphus, various silver coronets, and chalices, and rings, some ancient spurs, an iron helmet, and a wooden head. It was possible to carry them out as the fire spread.

The ruins were said to present the most affecting spectacle in the whole world. Few ladies could behold it without weeping. Many aged persons left their rooms for one last time to gratify a feeling of melancholy interest.

One melancholy man rose and stood and said that long after every one who knows and hears me shall have been laid low in the grave, the dismal tale of the Minster and its destruction shall be handed down, and that it will make the ears of your children's children tingle, and their children too, and so on, down the centuries, and he paused, and his audience listened, and then began to cough in the residual smoke.

As the clock struck three earlier that morning, Jonathan Martin made his way out through a hole in a window and into the night. It would be several hours before the fire was discovered, during which its devastation was preventable and its progress slow.

Dolbeine looked on and remained placid. Hutton endured its spread with characteristic equanimity. Sterne remained bored. Sewall's monument and Bowett's sepulchral shrine, still stood.

At half four a passer-by saw a light and decided workmen must be preparing a vault—this vault-digging tending to happen at night—and thought not to report it.

At five, several explosions were heard but not traced to their source. Those who heard these explosions and later testified openly to their doing nothing said it is hard to trace a bang after it is done, which is certainly true.

Archbishop Matthew was not yet deprived of his fingers and toes.

At around seven a lad named Swinbank was arriving for his choir practice, and being early, and finding the doors still locked, amused himself by doing slides along the ice. The choirboy fell on his back and, from that position, was looking directly upward at the roof. The smoke coming out of it was then noticed.

Dolbeine had not yet lost a finger.

Jonathan was on the road, heading northwest out of York. The man was feeling his hunger, having eaten nothing since the previous day and having worked very hard all night at his fire-making.

—Will you suffer your servant to starve after this hard night's work in your service?

—No, replied the Lord, seeing Jonathan now on his knees. There is plenty of snow lying upon the ground under thy feet. Take and eat it, and drink of it.

And Jonathan took it, and ate it, and drank the liquids the eating produced in his mouth.

The bundle he had taken from the Minster was also causing some bother, and he changed it from one hand to the other much lamenting the fact that he had left his stick at the house of William Lawn, the shoemaker, whose pincers he had stolen and used to cut his way out of the Minster window. This stick he might have used to swing the bundle over his shoulder. If I had my stick, Jonathan said to himself, I would carry this burden on one shoulder, and then on the next, and my life would be much easier for it. Jonathan was at the height of his complaining when, not ten yards after, he found a walking stick upon the ground in the middle of the road, which was a sure sign that this was the right road and he had chosen the perfect direction to walk in.

Meanwhile, the blaze had taken, and various people were assembled. Mr Scott, a builder, attempted to enter by the south door but was driven back. The smoke was dense and respiration was impossible, he said. A gentleman made it further, and got as far as the organ screen, but was compelled to retreat or face suffocation himself. By way of the vestry door access was gained to the choir about which the fire was spreading. One of the Minster engines—a rudimentary kind of water-projecting cart—was rolled inside and set to work on the place where the communion plate was kept, which is where the fire raged most intensely at that point in time. The tabernacle screen was at this spot burned to the ground and the whole was melted into one mass.

Archbishop Dolbeine had still not lost his finger.

As the engine played on the flames, those men not pumping it set about carrying all the cushions, the whole of which they saved, these cushions, carried by the armful, and all the books they could grab from the north side of the choir too, as well as some hangings pulled down a little too hastily, and the communion table—this took four of them—and the curious old chair by the altar which had stood there so long that nobody had risked setting their weight into it for decades.

The next effort was to move the brass eagle, which was difficult, owing to its weight, its proximity to the flames, and the fact of it being very hot to touch. The heat and the smoke drove them off several times, and some of the men looked to see if any cushions were still left or something else by which they could claim their usefulness and excuse themselves with as they left. Eventually, the upper part of the brass eagle was carried out by the vestry, and after much advancing and retreating, the lower part was taken out via the chapter house.

Jonathan was too far from York by now to see what was what and had stopped looking back to look if there was smoke for some hours already. The roof was yet untouched by the fire, however, and so if Jonathan had been able to see it, he would have been disappointed. The fire was still possible to contain, those with the engine felt if only there was a second engine to play against it from the other side.

Within minutes the situation of the fire was altered as it spread around the south west corner of the choir and reached the organ, which took off with an appalling noise, they said, that was occasioned by the action of the hot rising air upon the pipes.

Having reached Easingwold by around eight that morning, Jonathan walked from one Easingwold inhabitant to the next trying very hard to sell a copy of *The Life of Jonathan Martin*. This was the third edition, the one listed at sixpence but that Jonathan preferred to sell for a shilling. That particular copy he sold for twopence and got a pint of beer for it, as well as a penny roll for a halfpenny.

Here begins the account of Jonathan's last wandering binge, the facts of which—what pint and where it was had—have been recorded with unusual exactitude, the author feels.

More engines were assembled, and these came fairly quickly but were also entirely too late. They were brought in by the bells of St. Michael-le-Belfrey, a squat little church directly facing the Minster, declaring, by that proximity, the insatiable appetite of that establishment for audiences. Its only real claim to fame, and a pleasurable one at that, is its being the baptismal church of Guy Fawkes.

The Yorkshire Insurance Company engine was placed at the south door, and its pipes threaded inside the Minster to the organ that was still burning but had ceased the earlier and noisier stage of its destructions because the tubes of it were melted. The city engines then came, and were stationed here and there, and the barracks engine too, with Major Clark, several other officers, and a file of the seventh Dragoon Guards, who set about organising everything that was already organised.

By causes entirely not of their own making, the barracks engine was soon put *hors de combat*, for although in excellent condition and very well oiled, and polished, and painted, it was supplied with water from a plug in the Minster yard which was full of straw and horse shit and other foul substances, by which conveyance upwards the pipes were subsequently clogged.

A second engine was brought inside the Minster, from the other side to the place of the first, with the pipes carried over the northern tabernacle work, it not yet being destroyed. This engine did some half an hour's spraying, but then the roof above the organ was lit, at the centre knots of the arches, apparently—not that it matters all that much to specify, or that it was maple-wood which burned, and then fell, and did then begin to do some destroying by its falling. They retreated with the second engine to the inner region below the central tower and did some spraying from there.

Jonathan was now leaving Easingwood and making for Thirsk, which lies about ten miles further north.

This was a better walk because he now had his new stick to hold and hang his bundle from.

And he had eaten a halfpenny roll.

There is no record of a beer being had between Easingwood and Thirsk, nor was there necessarily a place where beer might be bought or begged. Given the length of this particular leg of the journey, and the thirst generated by the first beer, Jonathan must have been wanting another soon after he left Easingwood.

Looking back, if Jonathan had looked and been able to see that far, the spectacle at York was becoming less disappointing.

The account of the *Authentic Report* does become tiresome at this point, the author feels, having only so much patience for point-by-point hysterics. So, briefly, then, a horde of men made it to the roof, did some chopping away at it to protect the east window, and did some spraying there too, one of the engine tubes being long enough, and everyone on the ground looked on, and there were absolute hordes of them, and all felt, in unison, so the *Authentic Report* describes, that it was awful, and stupendous, and *impressive in the extreme*, and so on.

The engine was still inside, and the men still pumping at it were looking at the choir and thinking that it had the impression of a furnace, things being that far progressed, and when the scribe of the *Authentic Report* imagined them, this writer described them as *resembling beings of another world, rather than inhabitants of this material globe*. Their voices, as they shouted to their comrades for *water* and other assistance, so the report continues, fell in harsh and discordant tones upon the ear. They seemed enveloped in an atmosphere so dense that sound could not ordinarily travel, or have its usual tones. All inside was vivid, and beautiful, and inexplicably grand, and so on, the painted windows enhancing the effect by their reflection, etcetera, and by the sunlight that also made in. A number of bats *and other birds* burnt out of their quiet retreats, were seen flitting about, unable to find an outlet, and many perished in the flames.

The Archdeacon sent an express to the Mayor of Leeds requesting their two finest engines, and then a second express followed requesting their next two finest engines after that. Given the distance between York and Leeds and back, this request was more a question of form rather than use, as York felt Leeds owed them assistance, even if anything which came of it would always be too late.

At ten minutes past nine, a portion of the roof fell in with a tremendous crash, caused greater illumination of the surrounds and pushed smoke out of the towers above like exhalations.

This was about when Archbishop Sharp was covered over his head with debris.

And Archbishop Dolbeine lost his finger.

And Archbishop Matthew had his fingers and toes knocked off too and was otherwise mutilated.

The roof kept falling in until about half ten, the molten lead coming in torrents, apparently, to pool over tombs and tombstones with their inscriptions embossed on its underside.

Another engine arrived from Escrick Park, the seat of Paul Beilby Thompson Esq. M.P., who had offered his beautiful grey carriage horses to do the hauling, which did strike all stood about as very good of him, the man who would later be ennobled and become a Lord—this being another of the idiotic and enduring traditions of the land. Then, another engine from Tadcaster, and they made holes in the windows to spray through.

Around eleven came the spectacle of a man cut off on the roof by smoke and flame, his staircase filled with it too, and all communication downwards seemingly cut off. He called to those below to throw a rope, or so they judged from his frantic gesticulations, but it was impractical to do so—too high—which led eventually to his climbing over the battlement and descent by the water spout, this being suggested to him in various ways by the hundreds assembled and watching.

Some well-meaning but injudicious persons, fearing the spread of the fire still further, set to dismantling the various monuments in the side aisles. Admiral Medley's bust was torn down and dragged along perfectly needlessly, but that was all stopped and a sentry posted to dissuade further removals.

The sentry was replaced at intervals as it was only possible to stay in the side aisles for a few minutes at a time as they were heated completely through, and the vaults below were beginning to glow, and the limestone pillars themselves could be seen to disintegrate at their base.

The action of the water, which flowed about the choir, chancel and chapel floors, helped abate the action of the fire, together with the dragging out of all burning rubbish and those fallen beams that could be hooked and hauled from what was described as, *a lake of fire*, which lay at the centre of it all.

By noon, it seemed the fires would go no further, and the long work of spraying on them continuously as they diminished commenced.

This was when Jonathan reached Thirsk. Here, more luck was had in selling *The Life of Jonathan Martin* for sixpence, which was better than the twopence at Easingwold but still short of the shilling he felt himself owed. This afforded two penny rolls for three halfpence and five glasses of beer. That all gave him propulsion to Northallerton, where he arrived at three in the afternoon. This was not bad transit, though Jonathan complained he would have been there sooner but for the Spirit which told him to stoop down near hedges when coaches passed which slowed him somewhat.

By two in the afternoon the first two engines from Leeds arrived, and then the second two, the last engine thrown over as it turned into the Minster yard. One of the horses fell and was severely lacerated, and the man attending that horse when it went down was slightly injured too—he, like so many others, will remain anonymous.

There was only the work of cooling to be done. We only have the work of cooling to do, these men from Leeds were told in their sweat. Actually, it was cool enough inside for the curious to enter the nave and look about, even ladies, which was when one lady remarked, as was later recorded in the *Yorkshire Gazette*, about it being a worthy subject for John Martin. Little did she think, the *Authentic Report* points out with relish, that Martin's brother had occasioned the terrible conflagration.

Sentries were placed upon the Minster, and the whole of it was finally secured, which meant those growing crowds had nothing to do but fall at last into sadness, so it is claimed, that one of the finest cathedrals in the world had sustained such damage. There was gloom on every countenance. A sort of stupor appeared to pervade all ranks as the people of York and its visitors, too, were overcome by the greatness of the spectacle. The workmen continued to pull out burning parts of the roof, and the engines went on with their spraying, and as evening fell—or as the *Authentic Report* describes it—*as the shades of evening drew on*, it happened that, occasionally, *a fitful flash of lambent flame was seen struggling with the gloom*—further signs, the author feels, that finer language and higher feeling sit parasitic on destruction.

12

An estimate of 7,245 hogsheads were sent to the cathedral to be sprayed upon it—this being a type of barrel—and it is on record, too, that the wells by the Minster were entirely drained of their water. Several hundred men were subsequently paid a couple of shillings each for enduring it and for whatever they did, even the carrying of cushions or the destruction of monuments, and Major Yarborough, with his characteristic generosity, donated a full five pounds to procure refreshments.

At Northallerton, Jonathan visited himself on the brother of his first wife, who was out, fortunately, and so Jonathan made good work on his fifteen-year-old son. He asked for a room until eleven that night, which from three until eleven would allow eight hours' kip. When the boy's father and his mother appeared at seven that evening, Jonathan was woken and decided he'd better placate them by opening his bundle and producing the crimson velvet and silk he took from the Minster. Country folk like bright colours, and perhaps his wife would like to make a dress of it for their daughter.

When asked at his trial why he took all that material and carried it so far, Jonathan said that his eye was simply caught by the sight of it hanging around the Archbishop's throne and the pulpit, and that he took his razor and cut it down, fringes and all, and stood there, with the gold tassels too, and asked himself the same question, because he was at a loss what to do with the bundle, and thought them already very heavy. *Make unto thyself a robe, like David the King, and put the fringe at the bottom of it*, was the obvious reply, but that still left the problem of the tassels, and so he was told, *Put them upon your cap*.

When Jonathan first appeared before the magistrates in the Hall of Pleas, his answer was different, and Jonathan said that he took the fringe and the tassels and all the rest of it as a witness against him, to show that I had done it, he said, and that the burning was my work, with these, the only surviving materials once the extent of it was ash, and its walls disintegrated, and the rest of York too, most probably, leaning toward where the Minster once stood, all buildings displaced by its absence, like displaced souls before the pit.

Jonathan also said, at his trial, that because he had nothing but his wife's wedding ring to his name—this being the ring of his first wife, who was dead—he felt he needed it. Actually, it was a debt he was owed because when he was incarcerated for threatening the bishop, the owners of the Asylum took all his possessions but that ring and made him a pauper.

Having given the brother of his first wife the materials but not saying where they were from, Jonathan then persuaded him to buy eight copies of his *Life* for four shillings—which was really a bargain, and if the man had not sold them in three weeks, he would take them back, which made it a sort of loan, with insurance. The deal was set at three and sixpence, and the brother of his first wife then directed Jonathan to a coal cart going from a public house close by and that was destined for some coal pits, it being clear enough that Jonathan was in flight, for some reason, and would do better to keep moving, that and the man's desire not to have him stay any longer, having not seen Jonathan for months, and finding him much wilder, in aspect, than before.

The cart, which left at eleven that night, was driven by a small boy called John Wilson who put up with having a man embark and hide beneath a sack whenever another cart was passed. This did not prevent them from stopping at a public house along the way and Jonathan disembarking and taking some more glasses of beer, which is where the boy heard some mention of York Minster. They arrived at a pit in the neighbourhood of West Auckland by eleven the next morning. Jonathan left more or less immediately across country, had at least one more pint of ale—at Riding Mill—reaching Corbridge by the next day, at noon, where he had another pint. Jonathan was now near enough ninety miles from York, which wasn't a bad effort, given the state of the roads, and the state of him, and the times he lived in.

From Corbridge, Jonathan tramped to Codlaw Hall, which stands on its own and isolated on the north bank of the Tyne, four miles from Hexham. This was the home of Edward Kell, distantly related on his mother's side. Jonathan had appeared in a similar state eight years earlier following his escape from the Gateshead asylum. This time, he arrived in higher spirits, perhaps owing to the drink, but without his stockings. His boots were filled with water, and Jonathan wished, first of all, to wash his feet. He stood there with his bundle, or what remained of it, and his newfound stick and a fir branch that was budding at the end which announced, so he said, the arrival of spring.

Edward Kell listened as Jonathan told him, whilst washing his feet, that he had been hunted at York like a partridge, for what, he did not say, but he did ask Edward if he had to hand the third edition of the *Life*, to which Edward said *no*, which prompted Jonathan to produce a copy and read to Edward the dream written in it about the destruction of London, in which Jonathan saw its inhabitants tearing at each other's flesh, after which the Spirit took Jonathan to the banks of the river, and he did a bit of digging there and found seven sharp objects, including an axe, which Jonathan held, and as he held it, found St John the Baptist before him, and struck off St John's head with one blow.

—Then you are a traitor, said Edward Kell.

—That is what they called me at York, replied Jonathan.

Jonathan slept there two nights and on the first day visited the local poor and prayed with them. The Newcastle papers arrived on the second day and contained a notice offering a hundred pounds for his apprehension. That caused the people of Hexham to search all over, seeking a rather stout man of singular manners about five feet six inches high and between forty and fifty years of age, with red whiskers—or what the author would call sideburns—and above them upon his head, light hair cut close, residing as it did high above the temples, and coming to a point in the centre of the forehead.

This man usually wears a single-breasted blue coat with a stand-up collar and buttons covered with the same cloth, that and a black cloth waistcoat and blue cloth trousers, half boots laced at the front, and a glazed, broad-brimmed, low-crowned hat. At other times he wears a coat with yellow buttons or, when travelling, a large black leather cape coming to his elbows with two pockets within the cape—a curious detail, the author feels—and with a square piece of dark-coloured fur extending from one shoulder point to the other. Otherwise, a drab-coloured great coat, with a large cape and shortish skirts.

It is hard to imagine any of the people of Hexham and other such places paying too much attention to the various coats described. The crucial detail comes after—

The said Jonathan Martin is a Hawker of a Pamphlet entitled—following which the third edition of Jonathan's *Life* is described.

That is what did it, given Jonathan's trail of purchasers between York and Hexham, which was by far outnumbered by those who did not buy the *Life* as it was offered but recalled him too and turned out all their efforts to receive a hundred pounds for the man who had asked of them a shilling.

Perhaps the author will forego the exact details of Jonathan's capture and how the sheriff's officer tracked him down and burst in and found him and Edward Kell sitting there, and so on, because this isn't that kind of book.

13

I feared the terrors of hell stared me in the face, writes Jonathan in the *Life*, but was visited in a shrubbery, and He held a branch, and on it were two blossoms, and those blossoms were fruits. It was 1813.

Seizing my hand, he bore me through the forest, and we travelled like that till there was a ladder, which he ascended, and from which he fell after the seventh step, and I saw his wounds bleed, and I comforted Him.

Placing Him on the altar, I breathed to Him as He had once breathed to me, and the wounds dried, and the blood retreated.

This altar was a rock, and in it was a city, and below that city was a lake, and within that lake was all the liquid I had driven out of Him and freed Him of, and from which they now drank in that city and in that rock on which we lay, and I now rested, knowing that the city was at work beneath us and that we would smother it soon enough.

It was impossible that an unlearned man such as myself would be His instrument, but I was His instrument, and so the instrument speaks, knowing it by speaking it and speaking it to know it.

This especially so, given I had an impediment to my speech, but my impediment is His doing, and the cut is His work and His message, and my first lesson by the world.

I was alternately clouded with unbelief and hope for three days, after which two men called me in a loud tone of voice to the graveyard. I walked to that place and looked in, and just then, as I did so, the graves seemed to open and display their inhabitants, some reduced to skeletons, others newly interred.

They showed me a sepulchre in which the body of a man was just laid, and from his mouth came further raising of the dead, both small and great, every one of them provided with a short spade, myself excepted.

This world was not a resting place for me. I had to watch and pray until called to mingle with the spirits.

I was walking by the same churchyard, and it was filled with the most beautiful people that might be appreciated, all of them holding out their hands, and I held up my own, but there was flesh dropping from them and from my bones, and I wondered as I saw that how I felt no pain.

Looking up, they were gone, excepting a few now dressed in grave clothes who returned to the ground as if returning to sleep, I knew, with great happiness, that soon I would join them.

I had not yet felt the witness of the spirit that my sins were pardoned, and so it was that I went into the fields and knelt down and asked for a clearer display.

Birds in hedges have startled me as often as the devil has said, *people will think you mad.*

Overcome your slavish fear of the world, said he, for the Devil was a liar and a murderer from the very beginning.

Assail me with profane talk, I thought, and as many licentious songs as can be sung, and tell me this is the only means to communicate, and I will hold my cut with my tongue turned backwards and show it to be wrong.

I took the prayer books, learned all the words inside, and spoke them in church and sought to feel the connection between those words and His words, and felt nothing.

The first Love Feast I attended was at Yarm, but there was little feasting and not much love, and it was all about the ticket we brought, and did I have a ticket, and was it the correct ticket or was it expired, and how did my face look, and would the doorman let me in.

An old man came to me, and just before he did, several written letters passed into my vision, and I took one, and the old man dressed plainly asked me if I had got my letter, and I said, *yes*, that I had, which satisfied him, and so he went away.

After I joined the Methodists, I saw five moons in the firmament at one time. These were the five months.

I was asked again and over if I felt the *Witness of the Spirit*, and my reply was simple, that I did not and would not till the time came.

But at a different church, and when all had gone but the Minister, Curate, and Clerk, I was interviewed upon my outbursts and told them, by reply, of terrible dreams of Last Judgement, which satisfied their curiosity, and seemed to secure the Minister upon his decision, until the Clerk interrupted me and told his Reverence that I was an inoffensive man, and a good neighbour too, but I had lately been in the habit of hearing the Methodists. The Curate, who had just then entered the vestry, asked about what the matter was, and the Parson replied that it was *nothing but the cursed Methodists who had put this poor man out of his wits*. To which I could not help smiling, writes Jonathan.

He turned to me and said, *Poor man they have frightened you to death.* I replied by saying—*They have, and thousands besides, but it is a death unto sin and a new birth unto Righteousness.* After which, we parted.

I desired again to speak to the Clergyman. His lady, having heard of my being a drawer, sent for me in order to see some of them, and the two of them sat and looked as I spread them out, and both he and she approved, and each said what fine work it was, and how excellently I drew, and she said that she would dispose of them for me, *among the quality*, if I would but leave the Methodists.

The lukewarm state of the established church grieved me, and the more I reflected upon it, the more I felt impelled to instruct them of their danger, that orderliness is a kind of calcification, and that the races and card parties and balls and plays which they attended, were an expression of their confinement and the corruption of confinement, which sends its bodies out to find false pleasures and false amusements. I said that their pleasurable amusements were akin to the rotten parts of a building, which may be liquefying and might be subverting the whole but are still mere putrefaction.

On Friday a man held out to me a piece of honeycomb. On Saturday I gave away my working clothes. On Sunday I lay transfixed by the awful fact that the law prevents me from acting against the Establishment. On Monday I came out in opposition to both, seeing one as the other and each as one.

I prayed the Constable be deprived of his power to lay hold of me.

The Sunday following, I arrived at the church, but the doors were shut and locked. Thinking how to gain admittance, a voice spoke inwardly and said, *go round the church seven times*, which I did, and on the seventh circuit, the Clerk was there with his key, and I replied to his surprise saying, I am here to have the pleasure of viewing the monuments of the dead, which satisfied him, and he let me in. Afterwards he went to ring the bell, and in his absence,

I immediately took possession of the pulpit, in which I lay down, the door to it shut. I waited for the people so that I might deliver my message and free myself of their blood. The morning service began, and I fought against my desire to burst up and interrupt the prescribed and dead formality of their praying. And then my time came to speak, and I rose, and the Clerk took the role of Constable, and before I spoke had me by the leg, and pulled me with it from the pulpit, so all I managed were the words *let me go* and not the other words I had been preparing.

The Minister's wife came to see me after that and told me if I felt heavy I should read a play or an entertaining novel and that I would find relief by it, to which I replied that I put no confidence in such remedies.

I was at work as usual in the tan yard filling a cart with bark when I looked up and the clouds parted, leaving countless moons, and on one of these moons was written, UNDERSTANDEST THOU THIS.

Some days later, I was at work again, and, when looking up, saw as it were a great sword pass by in the air, twelve yards in length and the same distance from the ground.

At this time, I began writing letters to the Clergy, entreating them, if they valued their souls, to amend their lives and flee to the Blood of Sprinkling.

I lost my employment, and my friends would no longer come near me because of my zeal, and my brethren disowned me too, fearful I would endanger the cause. So it was that I came to be alone and had no fellowship.

One day, after a long journey, I was met with three stone images, an aged man, a woman, and a youth. The man stretched forth its hand and welcomed me, and it was a warm hand, and had the feeling of flesh and blood. The woman took my hand next, but the youth did not.

I found employment at Norton, but the wages they gave were not sufficient to keep my family. At Whitby, there was further employment, and the wages were better.

At Norton I preached again but was dragged out through the congregation, and so I took to writing some papers and posting them on church doors. But my admonitions were despised, and I was driven from that place by those whose eternal welfare was the sole object of my solicitude.

As I retreated, an Angel appeared and pointed to the church at Norton, and looking that way, I beheld a flame of fire ascending into the air, to which I approached, and was met by two men, each turning over coal in their hands, who went with me to a public house and got drunk before my eyes.

At Bishop Auckland, I was again expelled from its church, following which there was a flood, and I feared it would overwhelm me, but my Redeemer appeared and, touching a rock, turned it over, and the torrent was redirected.

At the village of South Church, which lies just outside Bishop Auckland, I spoke against the Minister, *thou hast no business in that pulpit, thou whitened sepulchre,* said I, *thou deceiver of the people,* and was dragged away once again, only this time I was arrested as a vagabond. The Clergyman appointed an attorney to write against me, and they wanted my employer at that time to swear that I was deranged, which he would not do. And so they enquired of my neighbours if they were afraid of me, and they said no. One dear woman said upon her interrogation, *I durst sleep with him all night and not be a pin worse,* and I was thankful for it, and told her so.

At this point, my wife became a great enemy to me, to which I said, we must deny all men, even wife and child, for the sake of Christ. Our positions were drawn and remained that way until she died eight years later.

She told me of her dreams and I denied them all, knowing myself the difference between a prophetic dream and a deranged one. In one of them, she was visited by a prodigious monster with an iron chain about its neck, which said, as it came towards the vicinity of her ear, *If thou let thy husband attend the Methodists, thou shalt have a hell upon earth whilst thou livest.*

She next said that she would stone me in the chapel and make an end of herself, and I prayed against it, and my prayer was heard because she did not stone me as she said she would, not there in any case.

About this time I heard that the Bishop of Lincoln or of some other place, but I think it most probably Lincoln, was to hold a confirmation at Stockton for the Bishop of Durham. Hearing that the first Bishop, though not necessarily the second, was a good man and an eminent Christian at that, I decided he would not fear death if that were so. My resolution was to try his faith by pretending to shoot him, for which I visited my brother William at Newcastle for the loan of his old pistol. Returning home, and with my wife seeing it, and asking after it, I told her it was to shoot the Bishop with, what else. In the morning the pistol was gone and I dropped the matter, and there it may well have ended were it not for some officious person who heard about it and told of it, and so it was that I was summoned by the Magistrate to account for myself.

—*I did not intend to injure the man,* is what I said in my defence, *though I consider they all deserve shooting.*

Jonathan Martin was taken into custody the next day and brought before the Justices at Stockton, which is where he was asked what he would have done had he found the pistol, to which Jonathan replied that it depended upon the circumstances and how well the Bishop answered his questions.

For his reply and following testimony of his various interruptions at church, Jonathan was sentenced to life in a madhouse.

In *The Life of Jonathan Martin* that pistol is described as an old broken-barrelled device, held together with string. If I had dared fire it, writes Jonathan, it would have blown my hand off. Let the reader judge me better by that detail.

14

Let my readers picture to themselves what a rational man must feel to find himself shut up for life in a madhouse, among madmen, and subject to the same treatment as if he himself were insane, writes Jonathan, and to add to the melancholy picture, have irons riveted on his legs, and his windows doubly barred, and to make assurance doubly sure, the walls of his prison raised so high that any attempt to get over them would be certain to break that man or that half of him which first met the earth.

That man I was, and I survived it too, defying the fall that would kill all others and spending my time as best I could, seeking out those confined with me who were equally sane and preaching at them for their betterment.

Much of that was again verbatim, the author notes, having not quite resolved against caring which was which.

It would be sufficient to assemble the book from verbatim quotes and nothing more, taking all interest in their reorganisation and the effects of that rearrangement, the author thinks, and the author wonders why that was not done and what desires lay behind this decision.

For the first month my keeper treated me with kindness and, perceiving no signs of lunacy which he would expect, set me to work in the fields. At night, I was shut up in a room with four others, all of them having filthy and disorderly habits. The room was so small we could not pass between our cots without straddling the bed with one leg and limping along the floor with the other.

My keeper and his wife went for a few days to Sunderland leaving charge of the house to their daughter, a servant girl, and myself. Returning drunk, we heard him come upstairs to inspect our room, and finding one of the cots damaged, he took a stick to correct the man he suspected. I fell between them because it was not this man but another who had done the damage, which enraged my keeper, who called me a heretic dog and confined us all in that small room for a month, during which we exchanged filthy habits and suffered greatly.

One was so mischievous he would pull me out of bed by the leg when I slept and swill the contents of the chamber pot over my head. We were otherwise cold and hungry.

The keeper did not come in but visited abuse upon us from the passage, and worse, until eventually he relented and took me down to the kitchen, confessing it was the drink which did it, and he would shave me, and I could be at liberty again.

About this time, Jonathan saw his wife standing upright, dead in the water, all surrounded by ice.

Jonathan is explicit in distinguishing dreams from occurrences. I dreamt this, he will write, or this is what I dreamt, or that was my dream. Less often, the word *vision* is used, a word that has application in both worlds. But where Jonathan is clear in demarcating his dreams, it is because those dreams, for him, were distinct realities in their own realm and had nothing to do with psychological effects. In the context of a present-day book, to identify Jonathan's dreams as such, to say this was his dream and that was his recollection would be mistaken. To use the word in an account of Jonathan's life falsifies Jonathan's experience, the author decided, because the word *dream* has now gathered up two centuries of psychological baggage.

Not long after, my keeper took against me again and chained me to my bed for a fortnight. The servant girl let it be known about town, and an order was sent that I be taken from the asylum at West Auckland to another at Gateshead.

Without having reckoned with my sores, I told the Constable I could walk, and so we set out and made some distance with me not wishing to mention them, but they delayed me, and eventually stopped all further progress. The rest of the journey was by the assistance of the Constable and two pit men, who, returning home from their labour, agreed to hoisting me and hauling my feeble self until we made our destination. It took many days until I retained full use of my limbs, after which I made myself useful to my new keeper at Gateshead, which moved him to pity and to providing some money to pay the coach fare for my wife and son to visit. I had become his gardener, waiter, baker, underkeeper, and, in short, his servant of all work, and felt happy in the conditions of my confinement.

Entrusted to such an extent that he had access to the garden key, Jonathan felt one morning, when digging and cutting and so on, that it would not hurt at all if he walked to a nearby castle to take it in, and then upon that walk, and being well underway, decided furthermore that it would not hurt if he went to visit some friends, and that when they received him, and saw him so very well entrusted that he could visit castles and such like, they would understand that his keeper did not think him mad either.

My friends at Hexham were much surprised and did not just ask about my upper lip, which I had recently stopped shaving. From there, I went to Norton, to visit the Magistrate, and show him the keys as evidence that I was not in fact mad at all and that it had been his mistake to sentence me to life in a madhouse. It was a hot morning, and I appeared before him covered with dust and sweat and explained, as he listened, how I was thought worthy by my keeper of having a degree of liberty, and so I must be worthy, and I should be at liberty. His worship seemed surprised, and I did admit that my upper lip was different to the last time we met and that I had not had the opportunity to shave elsewhere due to my long journey. The other Magistrates were gathered, or I was sent to where they already were, it was not clear to me which, and it was decided that my committal for life was indeed correct, and that I was wrong, and that I should be better secured from now on. And so I was returned and put in irons at Gateshead with the rivets set by a blacksmith. The keeper treated me very differently from then on, and I was no longer his gardener, waiter, baker, underkeeper, and servant of all work, but his prisoner.

I was chained to the bed at first, Jonathan writes, with another inmate who had the itch, and was soon infected, and my suffering, between that and the heat of the weather in so small a room filthy with vermin, was truly great.

My wife and child were denied access, which was a blessing because of the itch, but still a considerable source of unhappiness to me, with my poor boy turned away at the door.

That night, I heard a voice clearly address me by my name. Jonathan, it said, thy son shall speak to his enemies within the gates and will do so valiantly. Which lifted my spirits and the next day, when the keeper and a doctor came to inspect me, during which the doctor took notes, I said to them both, even though my body is chained to this bed and the windows are secured, *He* will release me, and put my enemies in confusion.

They asked me who *He* was, and I looked back a little confused myself, and then caught my wits and said, *my prophecy is realised.*

At last, my keeper released me from the bed, and arranged the fetters so that I could work, after which I was employed to wait upon the patients, the first of whom was a whole mass of wounds and ulcers—these I had to wash and dress—and that was when I became a doctor myself, and did what doctors do, or what I had seen them do often enough, which is to watch the ill and listless die. The man did die eventually, his flesh wasting away in corruption, only skin and bone remaining, which I saw as I administered his chief nutriment, oranges and port, keeping that of him going that was left. I awakened him to a sense of his miserable state by reason of his sin, and he cried for mercy, and his cry was answered, and he declared it so, though he lost speech soon after and died happy.

As soon as I was rid of him, they assigned me to another, and so it was that I saw several others die.

Otherwise, I was visited, and this was my role, to be visited, with inmates sent to my room when their conditions of thinking required my help, and I sat and listened to their profanities and replied as best I could to release them of their abuses.

The most awful spectacle, Jonathan reports, was that of a former innkeeper who died during one of his wicked fits and, given he was much in the habit of blasting his limbs, had to have his tendons cut to fit him in his coffin.

It was a curious fact that the inmate who caused Jonathan the greatest frustration by tearing at his clothes—*I had three shirts torn off me in less than a month*—would end up assisting him in his escape. The man, named Jack, was devilish in his madness and would throw live coals into the beds or push the inmates themselves into the fireplace if they passed before him and would engage in all other mischievous pranks he could think of. Jonathan came back to the room they then shared with the freestone he had found, and which he intended to use against his fetters, and looked at Jack and feared that Jack would give him away. His wife had been allowed a last visit that morning and had told him of the further advance of her sickness and left him with the words, *Pray for me, may God bless you, my strength is fast fading, and I fear that I shall be able to come no more*—which Jonathan used to propel him as he ground at the joint. As she lay dying, she sent a message to the keeper to please let Jonathan come visit her, which was refused, and that refusal, too, propelled Jonathan on with his grinding. She had sent their son, only seven years old, to do the pleading, hoping that his youth, innocence, and distress might soften their hearts. And she sent him again with her dying words, and the keeper's wife shut the door on his face, so Jonathan reports, and left Richard outside and bereft. Jonathan learned sometime after his escape that his wife was charged one shilling six pence a week to be waited upon by a woman who locked her in at night with no attendant but her child and that the boy was so greatly neglected that none would even cut his bread, and so he ate it by picking out the heart of the loaf and leaving the sides. These were the conditions that the boy, Richard, endured as he sat up with his dying mother each night. Jonathan had ground down the joint to a thread, and was ready to be released, but upon that moment, the keeper's wife found the grinding stone in Jonathan's room and took it away and told the keeper about it. The keeper was convinced that it was Jack who had picked the stone up and taken it there, and as he could not believe that Jack was capable of plotting, he thought no more about it. Jack was a frequent picker up of stones, Jonathan writes, which is how the keeper was fooled.

The details of his escape are there to be read in the *Life*. Anyone who reads it and feels the urge can write it up, and draw it out, and make something of the action.

As are the details of how the Magistrates finally decided to leave Jonathan alone, his accusers having died in any case, which Jonathan felt they justly deserved.

Nine years later at York, and facing his removal to Bethlem, Jonathan was thinking about his escape from Gateshead, certainly—and had all the raw content of it to hand. His memory of escape was important, in that context, having a vital function rather than one of entertainment.

At York he had no chance of making it into the ceiling and through the roof, as before, but would go up the chimney, which seemed to be progressing well until Jonathan reached that region of the chute where bars had been placed. Retreating back to his cell, the man waited urgently until the door was opened the next morning and rushed off to wash himself, hoping to conceal the evidence, the soot, which was all over his hands and elbows and draining from his nostrils and so on. That would be his last attempt. At Bethlem they were more used to such antics, and the complex was so big that escape from one quarter simply meant imprisonment in another.

15

The destruction of York Minster must be lamented *as an individual and personal bereavement*, declared the Lord Mayor.

Five thousand copies of the *Life* in its third edition were printed. The second and first editions were entirely disposed of.

Jonathan married a second time, and his wife, Maria, who was 20 years his junior, accompanied him on his travels. They lodged overwinter at York from 1828 to 1829, staying with William Lawn the shoemaker. Jonathan became well known, walking about town in his wide-brimmed hat and black leather cape—the one with fur from shoulder to shoulder—hawking his third edition to all who would be stopped. Otherwise, he set about affixing denunciatory letters to the doors of churches, which was something he now did, and was known to do.

—be a shamd of your selvs and wepe, for your Bottls of Wine and your Downey Beds will be taken away, is a line in one of these letters already quoted from.

Jona. Martin, a frind of the Sun of Boneypart Must Conclude By warning you again Oh, Repent repent He will soon be able to act the part of his Father.

This is how that letter ends, with the address included, *Aldwark No. 60*, a six-minute walk from York Minster.

The letter in question was found tied to the gates of the choir inside the Minster, or by another account, stuck on one of its spikes. The string that was used was a shoemaker's waxed thread. The Verger took it down and gave it to a Clergyman who subsequently ignored it, deeming the letter too absurd to take seriously.

The next letter, also preserved and already quoted from, was found by a sailor from Hull. When walking the western aisle with his wife, he saw it on the ground, near a pillar. It was wrapped in a small packet he first supposed contained something offensive, and that had been placed there by some frolicsome boys. Passing it again, and then again, the sailor eventually kicked it with his foot and finding it to be hard, unwrapped the thing, tied with a shoemaker's waxed thread—Lawn had lost a good amount of that to Martin, it seems—and wrapped around with old matting. The wrapped thing was a stone, and around that stone was a pamphlet entitled *The Life of Jonathan Martin*, and then a letter sealed with cobbler's wax and addressed to the clergy of York. The sailor read it to those at the house he was stopping in, and none thought it worth reporting.

A Just Warning far all Clargy of York whose Eyes stand out with Fatness and still caing mor mor wine, mor plum Puding, and Rost Beffe—

—Oh you Fools and Gready wolves your time is short and the Judgement of God is Hanging over your Giltey Heades—

—your torments will be ten thousent Fauld mor you Deserves, it goes on.

And then, *Belve me your time short, and For your wicketness God is about to cum out of his place to take vangins on you, and all those that obay your Blind Halish Doctren, for it Cums from the black reagens of the Damd*, and so on.

The address, *Aldwark No. 60*, is again there, in the margin, at the very edge of the letter.

A third letter was found somewhere else, nearby, and prophesied that the great churches and minsters would fall down on their guilty heads. Which is the next best thing in a country without mountains.

The fourth and fifth letters were lost.

On the Saturday Jonathan was observed perambulating about the Minster, inspecting it from all sides, but with particular attention directed at the western towers, or so it was reported.

On Sunday at eleven, he left Aldwark No. 60 for the last time, and the shoemaker lost no further waxed string to the prophet.

This time, Jonathan's wife, his second wife, Maria, would not intercede like the first had done, for though he told her of his plans and left her at Leeds to think it over, Jonathan took the precaution of stealing her wedding ring as she slept. I will only return your ring, Jonathan answered the morning after, if you keep my projections and my designs to your own self. This was all contradicted and denied by her after the fire, as it made sense for her to do, had Jonathan in fact done what he said he did, with the confession, the ring, and the supplementary vow he placed upon it.

Jonathan entered the south transept with his equipment, a razor with a white haft, the back of which he used instead of a steel, a flint, tinder, matches, and a penny candle cut in two. This candle would soon run out, but with it being Candlemas Day, there were plenty of candles to re-employ.

During the service the organ made such a buzzing noise, Jonathan recalled.

I thought, thou shalt buzz no more—I'll have thee down tonight.

After the service, during which he did much walking about, so the sexton noticed, Jonathan lay down behind a tomb.

The *Full and Authentic Report* suggests the monument of Archbishop Grinfield as Jonathan's most likely place of concealment. By which was meant *Greenfield*, the author suspects.

Archbishop Greenfield died in 1315. In 1735, his tomb was opened and a gold ring with a ruby was taken off his finger. This ring was never used to mark professions of faith or to seal letters—the bishop had another for that—but was wafted about to accompany the bishop's pontifications and remind those who saw it how this bishop, in particular, had a taste for finer things, and was terribly in debt. The bishop said that he was merely obeying the definitive fashion set by Innocent III, who ordained that the ring should always be gold, and solid too, and set with a precious stone on which nothing was to be cut.

Set the stone just as it was found, said Greenfield, and then wavered a little and asked for a polish here and there and another few minor refinements.

Reading about episcopal rings, the author finds that it is a common thing for bishops to be buried with their rings and then have those rings taken from their skeletal fingers and occasionally their thumbs. At York Minster alone, at least three have been retrieved, those of Archbishops Sewall and Bowet in addition to Greenfield's.

These rings were never worn on the forefinger since that digit signals silence, but were sometimes found on the middle finger, if not the annular. The right hand was also preferred, as it is the more distinguished of the two. The ring is the badge of fidelity, and the church is the bride.

Greenfield lost his other ring to the king who, according to custom, was entitled on the death of every archbishop and bishop to his best horse and palfrey, with saddle and bridle, a cloak with a hood, the bishop's cup with the ewer, a gold ring, of course, and the kennel of the hounds of the deceased. This list was an extension of the king's understandable caution that the seal of the bishop, if got into the wrong hands, might be used to falsify documents. If you are bringing me the ring anyway, you might as well bring it on a horse, and accompany that horse by hounds, and supply me with the bishop's own cup to drink from when it all arrives.

As the writer of the *Authentic Report* imagines him, Jonathan left his hiding spot and set about wondering what he would burn first, having nothing but burning on his mind. The ringers were in the belfry, and Jonathan watched them from another hiding place, perhaps a column, and observed that when they left, these ringers neglected to lock the door. This event gave Jonathan the opportunity to obtain the rope he escaped with, a bell-ringing rope, without which he would have been condemned to burn with the Minster or be found its prisoner by the first of its rescuers.

The Minster still had its own prison and could even carry out its own executions. Two inmates of that prison saw a light in the belfry after nine, they said, and a passer-by saw one after eight. That evening, Jonathan cut himself a ninety-foot section of rope, hauled it up through the floor, doubled it, and tied knots to make a ladder.

This rope was also used to get Jonathan over the iron gate and into the choir, which is where most of the flammables happened to be kept, such as the cushions and the prayer books. These he piled in two heaps, and lit, and made his escape.

Asked after if he felt fear during all these activities, Jonathan said *no*, and that he was, on the contrary, quite happy.

And I got a bit of praying done too, he added.

16

Looking upon the sea, I saw great hordes of men advance out of the waves. They came with fury and covered the Earth and England fled before them.

—I have observed many patients with *monomania*, and like Jonathan Martin, they have very tenacious memories and will not forget a thing, said a physician testifying at his trial.

I spoke against those who would not see it, and they filled my clogs with dirt and mire and then threw my boots into a well. Often it was that I stood with my feet wet and cold.

They led a pony about in the yard before me and gave a shout for the hounds. I told them it would never be ridden on a hunt, and they made sport and game with me, but sure enough by eight the pony lay dead before them.

—insane persons are generally very angry at attempts to prove them so, claimed another physician.

Next morning they said I was nothing but a witch, and not content to give me wet feet every day, they purchased stuff to put on my jacket neck. Some called it *Cow's Itch*, but I called it the *Devil's Itch*, for the more I scratched the more it itched and the more it itched I scratched. Had I not despised to dance with perfect hatred, I should have done so then.

—I have known the prisoner for five years. I am a fellmonger and live in Stillington. I worked four months with him two years ago and saw how cruelly he was treated. One day, when he was preaching on some steps, they poured blood on him.

—His eye was red, his pulse full, hard, strong, and quicker than usual, a third physician testified. He is not fit to go at large.

—I observed the appearance of a wound or accident on the frontal bone, declared a fourth. He has a voracious and inordinate appetite.

—I have had charge of Jonathan Martin, said the keeper of his prison, and have seen a good deal of him. The man walks thirty miles a day in his yard. He was highly exasperated when he learnt the kind of defence which his brother intended. He said that he had a great many enemies—the blackcoats were against him. He supposed that they wanted to prove him by himself, but that could not be, as God would not have taken a madman to do his work.

—I have heard him say that rather than own he had done wrong, or think so, he would place himself before a cannon, and himself apply the match, added the jailor.

In summing up, the judge dwelled much on the letters of Jonathan Martin, declaring that they clearly showed a *diseased understanding*.

The jury took ten minutes.

I placed my feet on the fender and my accuser asked me if I was cold, and I said *yes*.

A man stood by me with a bow and a sheath of arrows and fired one of those arrows at the Minster door. This is what I saw, he said. I wished to shoot, and the man gave me the bow, and I shot but hit a stone.

By another account of what Jonathan said, he struck the stone because of people crowding about so that he could scarcely use his arm.

I next saw a black cloud come down to rest on the cathedral, and then it rolled over to the house in which I slept, and the cloud made the whole of it tremble. The house was so shook, he said, I was awoken from my sleep. It resembled the pillar of smoke and fulfilled the prophecy of Joel that God would pour out his Spirit upon all flesh, and the old men should see visions and the young men dream dreams, and that there should be signs in the heavens, blood, and fire, and vapour and smoke.

Here, Jonathan stopped abruptly, and when asked if he had anything more to say, he replied, *no*.

Jonathan had by no means the appearance of a *stout man* as described in the bill. And his *red bushy whiskers* were not at all prominent.

When he got back into the low room, he resumed his seat by the fire and sat for some time with his eyes closed, as if he was asleep.

At the Gateshead asylum, Jonathan sat on the floor, it was claimed, with two cross sticks as if he were fiddling. He called his sticks an imitation of David's harp. Some days he would have to be confined in order to be shaved.

A speech was given to the citizens of York following the fire—*I read a letter lately in a London paper*, it begins, purporting to have been written by an eyewitness in York, in which it was stated that, while the high and middle classes were actively employed in saving the Minster, and showed great sympathy, the lower orders looked on with apathy. This is a libel on the citizens of York, for the fact is quite the reverse, and there was but one feeling evinced, and there was, indeed, no distinction between high and low—with the audience crying, *none, none*, and otherwise agreeing profusely.

Or so it was recorded in the *Authentic Report*. And so too that all felt similarly moved, and there was no division, and all lamented equally the injury done to those *magnificent piles*—meaning, the Minster.

As Jonathan might have observed, this shared feeling condemned them equally too. Or, to put it more precisely, it showed, if true, that all were suffering from the same condemned order, that they were all, equally, servants of the Establishment. Shared misery at the loss of a so-called national treasure, of a noble pile, the capacity for a nation, or even just a city, to come together and unify around such an event, to become stupid with it, to share soothing and flattering lamentations of their collected loss, the historic calamity, demonstrates just how securely yoked these inhabitants are, how enslaved they must always be even at their most divided to a national myth, to the order of things, to stasis.

I bore no ill-will to any of them individually, said Jonathan when asked of his feelings towards the clergy, but merely to the edifice they serve.

When it was announced at court that Jonathan Martin stood accused of having *unlawfully, maliciously, and wilfully* set fire to the Cathedral Church of York, the accused objected only to the word *maliciously*—not maliciously, he shouted out. The author finds it necessary to record this detail and make a point of it.

My fifth letter was a very severe one, Jonathan said at his trial, and it was a shame the letter was lost because Jonathan had collected in it, so he said, all the curses of the Scripture. He was disappointed, he added, that he never received any reply from the clergy, even though he was good enough to sign off with the shoemaker's address at No. 60 Aldgate, by which he presumably meant Aldwark.

At York prison, Jonathan experienced extraordinary visions, such as when two angels came to visit him, one telling him to apply his lips to the tip of his wings, which he did, and being so attached, was carried beyond the walls.

When the doors of the court opened at eight, a tremendous rush took place. Anxious to see Jonathan Martin, to behold the man who would destroy the edifice, they crowded in, many well-dressed women among them too, who seemed to take their share in the pushing and struggling. The accused was placed in the dock and seemed perfectly unconcerned about his situation.

—*His countenance was perfectly placid, it wore no traces of terror, and certainly none of guilt.*

On the contrary, the *Authentic Report*, continues, *a smile played occasionally round his lips.*

The time will come, and they will flee to the mountains, the clergy first of all. And the sword, which expanded and flew at moon day, will reach them, and I will clean out my clogs and walk myself undisturbed.

If one can chase a thousand, two shall put ten thousand to flight, and three will end it all. I am the first and seek my second.

Our souls will tread the desert through with undiverted feet, wrote Jonathan. And even at this last moment, my tongue will not cease its movement. Being cut from its floor, it shall run with them.

www.ingramcontent.com/pod-product-compliance
Lightning Source LLC
Chambersburg PA
CBHW020534080526
44583CB00013B/853